TRUST ME, I'M DR. OZZY

TRUST ME, I'M DR. OZZY

Advice from Rock's Ultimate Survivor

OZZY OSBOURNE

with

CHRIS AYRES

GRAND CENTRAL
PUBLISHING

NEW YORK   BOSTON

Grand Central Publishing
Hachette Book Group
237 Park Avenue
New York, NY 10017

www.HachetteBookGroup.com

Printed in the United States of America

RRD-C

First Edition: October 2011
10 9 8 7 6 5 4 3 2 1

Grand Central Publishing is a division of Hachette Book Group, Inc. The Grand Central Publishing name and logo is a trademark of Hachette Book Group, Inc.

The Hachette Speakers Bureau provides a wide range of authors for speaking events. To find out more, go to www.hachettespeakersbureau.com or call (866) 376-6591.

The publisher is not responsible for websites (or their content) that are not owned by the publisher.

Library of Congress Cataloging-in-Publication Data

Osbourne, Ozzy, 1948–
    Trust me, I'm Dr. Ozzy : advice from rock's ultimate survivor / by Ozzy Osbourne. — 1st ed.
        p. cm.
    ISBN 978-1-4555-0333-9 (regular edition) — ISBN 978-1-4555-0724-5 (large print edition)   1. Osbourne, Ozzy, 1948–   2. Rock musicians—Health and hygiene.   3. Health behavior.   I. Title.
    ML420.O825A3 2011
    782.42166092—dc23
    [B]
                                                                                2011022443

Warning:
Ozzy Osbourne is not a qualified medical professional
Caution Is Advised

Seriously, Caution Is Advised

Disclaimer

Some names and personal details in this book
have been changed for privacy reasons, and most
questions have been edited.

Facts in the pull-out boxes and quiz sections were supplied
by Dr. Ozzy's research department (he's called Chris),
as Dr. Ozzy's memory of events between 1968
and the present are not entirely reliable.

This book should not be relied upon for medical purposes.

Important Safety Information

Do not use DR. OZZY if you suffer from medical conditions, ailments, or other health concerns, as this may cause sudden and unsafe death or death-like symptoms. Discuss your mental health with a qualified psychiatrist if you're considering using DR. OZZY. In the rare event that use of DR. OZZY results in the growth of winged testicles, seek immediate medical help, or fly to your nearest hospital. If you are under the age of 18 or an extraterrestrial lifeform, you should not use DR. OZZY. Trials have shown that a low dose of DR. OZZY is no safer than a high dose of DR. OZZY. Even trace amounts of DR. OZZY, which may be undetectable to the human eye, can result in serious damage to wildlife. If you suspect the presence of DR. OZZY, inform government agencies immediately and remain indoors. Use of DR. OZZY is legally prohibited in many territories and may be considered a felony in the United States. If accidental use of DR. OZZY should occur, wash the affected area immediately. DR. OZZY should not be taken with other self-help products, as confusion and bleeding could arise. Users of DR. OZZY have reported instances of cranial detonation, self-amputation, and madness. It is not possible to determine whether these events were directly related to DR. OZZY or to other factors. DR. OZZY does not protect against sexually transmitted diseases, ingrowing toenails, and bovine spongiform encephalitis. The most frequently observed side-effects of DR. OZZY include hysteria and indigestion. Less commonly, leprosy may occur. Also, in clinical studies of DR. OZZY, a small number of men experienced certain sexual side-effects, such as penis detachment and ocular ejaculation. These occurred in less than 99.9% of men and went away in those who stopped using DR. OZZY because of other, more serious side-effects, such as prolonged agony and screaming.

(Hazardous) Contents

DR. OZZY'S MEDICINE CABINET

Essential Items for All Patients

Description:	Use(s):
Black Stuff, Greasy (From Dad's Shed)	Acne/Blemishes
Brandy (4 Bottles)	Hangover
Brick (1)	Various
Cocaine, Eighties-Vintage (Bag Of)★	Athlete's Foot
Dynamite (2 Sticks)★	Constipation
Chicken (1, Alive)	Hangover (Severe)
Football (1, Leather)	Diagnostics
Lemon (1)	Common Cold
Sewing Kit (Stolen From Sister)	Surgery
Shotgun (Semi-Automatic)★	As Above
Pool Cue (1)	Diagnostics
Stink Bombs (Novelty Pack Of)	Indigestion (Severe)
Warm Vegetable Fat (Tub Of)	Earache
Whiskey (2 Bottles)	Anything

*Might not be legal where you live

The Doctor Is In...*sane*

Introduction

——

A Note to All Patients

If someone had told me a few years ago that I'd end up writing a book of advice, I'd have punched them in the nose for taking the piss. I mean, unless the advice is how to end up dead or in jail, I'm not exactly qualified. I'm Ozzy Osbourne, not Oprah fucking Winfrey.

But here I am: "Dr. Ozzy," as people call me now. And to be *totally* honest with you—I love this new gig.

I suppose it all started just before my last world tour, when a bloke from *The Sunday Magazine* in London came over to my house and asked if I wanted to be their new "health and relationship" columnist. When I'd finished spitting out tea over my Yorkshire terrier, I asked him, "Are you *sure* you've got the right person?" He said yeah, they were sure. If I wanted the job, the guy added, readers would write in with their problems—everything from stubbed toes to tearaway kids and fall-outs with the in-laws—and I'd give my answers. I wouldn't even have to put pen to paper: someone would call

me up every week so I could dictate my words of wisdom
over the telephone.

"Look—are you *absolutely 100 per cent sure* you've got the
right person?" I asked him again.

He just smiled.

The funny thing is, the more I thought about it, the more it
made sense in a crazy way. I mean, by all accounts I'm a medical miracle. It's all very well going on a bender for a couple of
weeks, but mine went on for the best part of 40 years. At one
point I was knocking back four bottles of cognac a day, black-
ing out, coming to again, and carrying on. Meanwhile, during the filming of *The Osbournes*, I was shoving 42 different
types of prescription medication down my neck every single
day. Each one of those drugs had about twenty or thirty different side-effects, so at any time, there were about a thousand
things wrong with me just thanks to the pills. And that was
before the dope I was smoking in my "safe" room, away from
the cameras; or the crates of beer I was putting away; or the
speed I was doing before my daily jogs around Beverly Hills.
I also used to get through cigars like they were cigarettes. I'd
smoke 'em in bed. *"Do you mind?"* I'd ask Sharon, as I lit up a
Cuban the size of the Red October. "Please, go ahead" she'd
say—before whacking me with a copy of *Vanity Fair*.

Of course, I've also taken a few...well, not-exactly-legal
things in my time. There are probably rats in U.S. Army
labs who've seen fewer chemicals than I have. What's amazing is, none of that dodgy shit ever killed me. On the other
hand, maybe it shouldn't be such a surprise, given all the other
things I've also survived: like being hit by a plane (it crashed
into my tour bus when I was asleep with Sharon in the back);
or getting a false-positive HIV test (it turned out that my
immune system was knocked out by booze and cocaine); or
a suspected rabies infection (after eating a bat); or being told
that I had Parkinson's disease (it was actually a rare genetic

tremor). I was even put in the loony bin for a while. "Do you masturbate, Mr Osbourne?" was the first thing the guy in the white coat asked me. "I'm here for my head, not my dick!" I told him.

Oh, and yeah, I've been dead twice: it happened (so I'm told) while I was in chemically induced coma after I broke my neck in a quad bike accident. I've got more metal screws in me now than an IKEA flatpack—all thanks to the amazing doctors and nurses at the NHS.

I always used to say that when I die, I should donate my body to the Natural History Museum. But since accepting the job as Dr. Ozzy—which snowballed into a gig at *Rolling Stone*, too— I don't have to any more, 'cos a bunch of scientists from Harvard University offered to take sample of my DNA and map out my entire "human genome." "What d'you wanna do *that* for?" I asked them. "To find out why you're still alive," they said. Thanks to them, I now know for sure that I'm a "genetic anomaly"—or at least that's what they told a room full of mega-brains at TED-MED, a medical conference in San Diego, California, when they announced the results in 2010 (see chapter 7).

The fact that I'm still alive ain't the only reason why I decided to become Dr. Ozzy, though. I've also seen literally *hundreds* of doctors and shrinks over my lifetime—and I've spent well over a million dollars on them, which is fucking ridiculous—to the point where I'm convinced that I know more about being a doctor than some doctors do. And it's not just 'cos of the insane lifestyle I've led. I'm also a terrible hypochondriac. I'll catch a disease off the telly, me. Being ill is like a hobby. I've even started to diagnose my own diseases with the help of the Internet (or I should say my assistant Tony, who does all the technical stuff, 'cos I ain't exactly Stephen fuckHawking when it comes to using a computer).

Of course, the question I always get is, "If you're such a hypochondriac, Ozzy, how could you have taken all those drugs over the years?" But the thing is, when you have an addictive personality like mine, you never think anything bad's gonna happen. It's like, "Oh, well, I didn't do as much as so-and-so: I didn't drink as much as him, didn't do as much coke, etcetera, etcetera…" Now, that might be fine in theory, but in my case, the "so-and-so" was usually a certified luna- tic like John Bonham. Or, even worse, Mel Gibson. Which meant they'd put enough up their noses to blast off into outer fucking space. Another thing I'd always tell myself was, "Oh, a doctor gave me the drugs, and *he* must know what he's doing." But that was ignoring the fact that I'd administered the stuff myself, usually at five hundred times the recom- mended dosage. It's honestly a miracle I didn't end up like Michael Jackson, or any number of other tragic rock 'n' roll cases. In fact, my friends knew me as "Dr. Ozzy" for years before I started giving advice professionally, 'cos I was like a walking pharmacy. I remember in the 1980s, a good mate of mine came to me for help with his leg ache, so I went to get my "special suitcase," pulled out a pill the size of a golf ball, and said, "Here, take one of these." It was Ibuprofen, before you could buy it over-the-counter in Britain. He came back a few hours later and said, "Wow! Dr. Ozzy, you cured me!" The only problem was that I gave him enough to cure an elephant. The bloke didn't shit or sleep for two months.

He didn't thank me so much for *that*.

But it ain't just medication I've given to my friends. As insane as it sounds, a lot of people have come to me for family advice. I suppose it's 'cos they saw me raising Jack and Kelly during *The Osbournes*, and they think I'm like an undead Bill Cosby or something. They ask me stuff like, "How do I get my kids to have safe sex?" or "How do I talk to them about drugs?" I'm happy to help the best I can. The only trouble is, when I talked to *my* kids about drugs, it was, (a) "Where's your stash?" and (b) "Can I have some please?"

I've become a better father since then. I mean, during the worst days of my addiction, I wasn't really a father at all, I was just another one of Sharon's kids. But I'm a different person now: I don't smoke, I don't drink, I don't get high—or least not on anything but endorphins from the jogging machine. Which means I enjoy my family more than ever: not just my five amazing kids (two of them to my first wife), but also my five grandkids. Plus, after thirty years, my marriage to Sharon is stronger than ever.

So I must be doing *something* right.

When you live full-time in Los Angeles, like I've done for the past few years, you often feel that people spend so much time trying to save their lives, they don't *live* them. I mean, at the end of the day, we're all going to die, one way or another. So why kill yourself with worry?

For me, though, the decision to change my life wasn't really about my health. It was about the fact that I wasn't having fun any more. As I used to say, I'd put the "wreck" into recreation. I was on Ambien, Klonopin, temazepam, chloral hydrate, alcohol, Percocet, codeine—and that was just on my days off. But morphine was my favourite. I didn't do it for very long, mind you. Sharon would find me passed out on the kitchen floor with the dog licking my forehead, and she put a stop to it. And thank God she did: I'd have kicked the bucket a long time ago otherwise. But it was tobacco that really put me over the edge. I'm a singer, that's how I earn a living, but I'd get a sore throat, then cough my way through a pack of Marlboro full-strength, to the point where I had to cancel gigs. It was ridiculous; the stupidest fucking habit you could ever imagine. So cigarettes were the first thing I quit, and that started the ball rolling. Now I take drugs only for *real* things, like high cholesterol and heartburn.

I can understand—sort of—if people think it's more

rock 'n' roll to die young. But what really winds me up is when you hear, "Oh, my great-aunt Nelly smoked eighty cigarettes a day and drank sixteen pints of Guinness before going to bed every night, and she lived until she was 103." I mean, yeah, that happens. My own gran lived until she was 99. But the odds ain't exactly on your side. Especially not when you get to the age of 62, like me.

Another thing that puts a bee up my arse: people who never get check-ups, and never go to the doctor, even when they're half-dead. It ain't macho—it's fucking pathetic. I had my prostate checked just the other week, for example, 'cos I'm on a three-year plan for prostate and colon tests. I couldn't believe how many of my male friends said to me, "Your prostate? What's *that*?" I was like, "Look, women get breast cancer, and blokes get cancer of the prostate." One guy even asked me, "Where is it?" I told him, "Up your arse," and he went, "So how do they check that then?" I said to him, "How do you think they check it? It starts with a rubber glove and ends with your voice rising ten octaves."

My prostate guy here in California says that every man over the age of 50 will develop some kind of prostate problem as they get older, but only half will get tested. And yet nowadays you can cure prostate cancer, no problem at all, if you get to it early enough. It's the same with colon cancer. Don't get me wrong: I'm the first to admit that the preparation for the colon cancer test ain't exactly glamorous. They give you this horrendous liquid to drink, then you have to crap through the eye of a needle until your backside is so clean, if you open your mouth, you can see daylight at the other end. But it's only 'cos I got tested for colon cancer that my wife did the same—and her test came back positive. Thanks to that, they caught the cancer in time, and she's alive today. That's a huge deal. So when I first became Dr. Ozzy, my first message was:

"Don't be ignorant!" To men, in particular, I wanted to say: I don't think a doctor's never put his finger up a bloke's ass before. They do it every day, so get over yourself. Besides, what would you rather have, a strange man's finger up your arse on a Monday morning—or the sound of a pine box being nailed shut over your head?

Having said that, every case is different—which I realized very quickly when I became Dr. Ozzy. For example, after reassuring my readers that they had to nothing to fear from dropping their trousers in front of their GP, I got an e-mail from a guy called Geoff in London.

He wrote:

Dear Dr. Ozzy:

After hurting my rear-end end while squatting down to tile a floor, I asked my GP to take a look at it. He ummed-and-ahh'ed for a while, then sent me off to a local teaching hospital, where a very excited specialist said he need to perform an examination. After giving me one of those back-to-front robes to wear, he lay me down on a slab on my side, and proceeded to round up some 20 junior doctors, who then took turns to file past my exposed behind, scribbling notes and snapping photographs as they went. Their verdict after that what seemed like ten lifetimes? I had a rare "perianal haematoma"... which would go away by itself.

All I can say is: sorry, Geoff. If it's any consolation, I once mooned a crowd of about half a million people at a gig, so you certainly don't hold the world record for having the largest number of people gazing up your asshole at any particular time. That one belongs to *me*.

★   ★   ★

To be honest with you, I can still hardly believe the stuff people write to me about. One guy asked if he should cut down on his cocaine use—'cos he'd just found out that he had high cholesterol. Another time, a girl in America—she was 22—asked if it was okay to sleep with her mum's (younger) boyfriend, or if that would make things weird at family get-togethers. I mean, what's *wrong* with these people? And as you'll see when you read on, that ain't even the half of it. Sometimes even Dr. Ozzy is lost for words.

When it comes to routine stuff, though, I pretty much always know the right answers. That's the thing about being a worrier, especially a worrier who's a hypochondriac: you end up investigating every last ache and twinge, so over time, all these random facts end up sticking in your head. If only I could remember *lyrics* so easily.

I wasn't always a such hypochondriac, mind you. When I was growing up in Aston, for example, our family GP was a guy called Dr. Rosenfield, and I'd do anything to get out of an appointment with him—mainly 'cos his receptionist was a woman with a full-on beard. I ain't kidding you: a big, black, bushy beard. It freaked me out. She was like Captain Pugwash in a frock. And Dr. Rosenfield's office was so gloomy, you felt worse coming out of that place than you did when you went in. As for Dr. Rosenfield himself, he wasn't really a bad guy, but he wasn't exactly a comforting figure, either. I remember falling out of a tree one time when I was stealing apples: I hit a branch on the way down, and my eye swelled up like a big black balloon. When I got home my old man smacked me around the ear before sending me off to get my injury looked at—then Dr. Rosenfield smacked me around the ear, too. I couldn't believe it.

I rarely got any kind of proper medical care in those days. If one of the six Osbourne kids had an earache, they'd get a spoonful of hot vegetable fat down their earhole. That was the done thing. And my gran would give us milk and mutton fat for bronchitis. As for my father, he had this tin in his shed, I don't know what it was, some kind of black greasy stuff, and if you got a boil on your neck he'd go, *"I'll get rid of that for yer, son, heh-heh-heh,"* and he'd slap it on there, and you'd be like, "NOT THE BLACK TIN! NOOO!" But that's all my folks could afford. Shelling out on zit cream from the chemist wasn't gonna happen when they could barely afford to get food on the table.

My father was one of those people who'd never see a doctor. He'd never take a take off work at the factory, either. He'd have to have been literally missing a limb to call in sick—even then, he'd probably just hop into the factory, like nothing had happened. I don't think he got a single check-up, right up until the end of his life—and by that time, he was riddled with cancer. His prostate gave up first, though. I don't know why he'd avoided doctors—it was all free on the NHS—but it made me think the opposite way. My logic is, if I go to the doctor now, and there's something wrong with me, they'll catch it, and I'll get to live another day. Don't get me wrong: I ain't afraid of dying. Although it would be good to know *where* it's gonna happen, so I could avoid going there....

Sometimes I think people in Britain don't make enough use of the NHS, because they're too busy complaining about it. But Americans—who'll queue up outside a sports arena for three days just to go to a free clinic—can't believe the deal we Brits get. I'll never forget the first time I got an X-ray done in the US after my quad-bike crash. The doc came into the room, holding up my slide, and whistling through his teeth. "How much did all that cost you, huh?" he asked, seeing all the rods and bolts holding my neck and back together. "A couple of mill? Three, four? Are you still getting the bills?"

"Actually, it was free," I told him. "I had the accident in England."

I almost had to call for a nurse, he got such a shock.

If you're a celebrity, mind you, medical care in America is just incredible. Too much so, if you're an addict like me, because they'll hand out pills like you're in a shopping mall. Whenever I do a gig in the US, for example, I'll always have a doctor check me out before the show, and in the bad old days, I'd score just about anything I wanted off those guys. At one point I basically just bought my own doctor and installed him in my house, salary and everything. It was magic until Sharon got wind of it. In England, I used to have to make up a backache, or hit myself over the head with a lump of wood, if I wanted to get a Vicodin. In America, all I had to do was say the word. It stopped only when the doctors realised that they had to answer to the Voice of God—ie, my wife.

"If you give him ONE more dodgy pill, *you'll* be the one who needs a doctor," she'd say.

To be fair to the American doctors, they do come up with some mind-blowing technology. I just had my eyes fixed with Crystalens surgery, for example. I'd suffered from cataracts for years, and my vision was so bad it was starting to give me problems on stage. So what they did was, they took out my natural lens—which was all fogged up—and replaced it with this bionic one, which can focus by itself. Left eye first, then the other a week later. It's amazing. Just unbelievable. No pain, for starters. And now I can read again. I see over there, over here, it's just fucking incredible. I've no idea how much it cost—probably eight tours, or something—but it's changed my life, totally.

I'm a new man now, in so many ways. I might be 62, but I haven't felt so young since the 1960s. Aside from my eyes, the other big change in my life is that I've pretty much become a vegetarian. Seriously. It's my new phase: brown rice and vegetables. I don't even drink milk, apart from a splash in my tea. And no, it ain't because of the *animals*. I mean, I used to work in a slaughterhouse, killing 200 cows a day. I ate a bat, for fuck's sake. You won't see me marching over the frozen tundra, hunting down seal-clubbers. I just can't digest meat anymore. I finally gave it up a few weeks ago, after I went out for a steak with my friend Zakk Wylde. I might as well have sealed my arse with cement, 'cos I couldn't crap for a week. I love the taste of beef, but it ain't worth it.

I ain't into any of that organic bollocks, either. People think they're buying another day on this earth when they pay for that stuff, so they get ripped off. If you want organic, grow your own, man. I used to when I was married to my first and we had a little cottage in Ranton, Staffordshire. A veggie patch also happens to be a great place to hide your stash of drugs. Having said that, I'd always get stoned and forget where I'd buried the stuff. One time, I spent a whole week down the garden, trying to find a lump of Afghan hash. The missus thought I was just really worried about my carrots.

I suppose when people hear stories like that, they might think I'm too much of a bad example to give advice. I wouldn't argue—and I'd hate for anyone to think, "Oh, if Ozzy survived all that outrageous behaviour, then so can I." But d'you know what? If people can learn from my stupid shit without having to repeat any of it; or if they can take some comfort from the crazy, fucked-up things my family has been through over the years; or if just hearing me talk about colonoscopies makes them less embarrassed about getting tested for colon cancer, that's more than enough for me: Dr. Ozzy's job will be done.

One last thing: being a hypochondriac, I would *never* tell someone to just stop worrying and/or come back later if their symptoms got any worse. That's bollocks, in my book. As I've always warned my own doctors: "One day you're gonna be standing at my graveside, and while the priest is reading out the eulogy, you're gonna look down and see the inscription on my headstone. And it's gonna say—'*See? I TOLD you I was fucking ill!!*' "

How to Cure (Almost) Anything

1

You'll Never Be Ill Again... Probably

If there's one thing I've learned as Dr. Ozzy, it's that everyone wants to be cured immediately—or better yet, three days ago. Luckily for the people who come to me with their problems, I'm exactly the same way. I mean, why go to all the trouble of a low-carb diet, if you can get rid of your gut with a needle and a suction pump? Or why take it easy after an injury, when you can pop a few pain pills and carry on?

As far as I can tell, there's only one drawback to quick fixes: THEY DON'T FUCKING WORK. Either that, or they sort out whatever's bothering you, but create another ten problems along the way. Take sleeping pills. For years I had trouble getting any shut-eye, so I started using a popular brand of sleeping medication. Before I knew it, I'd forgotten everything since 1975. The trouble was, my body built up an immunity to the drugs so quickly, I ended up necking a whole jar of the stuff just to get five minutes of rest. That's when my memory blackouts started, along with a bunch of other crazy side-effects, like wandering around the house stark naked at two in the morning.

What I should have done was find out *why* I wasn't sleeping—maybe something was making me anxious—and gone after the cause, not the symptom. But it's human nature, isn't it? We're all tempted by the cheap 'n' easy botch job, even though we know it ain't gonna last. That's why I've dedicated this chapter to "instant" cures: urban myths, old wives' tales, and unlikely stories I've picked up on the road...Some of them have worked for me in the past. Others are bullshit. I'll let you decide which is which.

Dear Dr. Ozzy:
What's the best cure for a hangover, in your (considerable) experience?
Justin, London

This is an easy one: have another pint. You'll be feeling much better in no time. It took me 40 years of trying everything and anything to make the morning-after feel better—short of actually giving up booze—until I finally realised that the only thing that ever worked was just to get shitfaced again. Like a lot of things, it was obvious in hindsight.

Dear Dr. Ozzy:
Help! I've got a cold. How can I get rid of it ASAP?
Tony, Boston

Funnily enough, getting loaded is also a great cure for the common cold. For example, I used to have this magic recipe for a "Hot Ozzy" (as I used to call it). You take two pints of whiskey, boil it up on the stove, add a bit of lemon—it's very important, the lemon—then drink it as quickly as you can. Trust me: by the time you've downed a Hot Ozzy, you won't just have forgotten you're ill, you'll have forgotten your own name.

Dear Dr. Ozzy:
I've been told that the easiest way to treat athlete's foot is to pee on your toes—because the chemical in anti-fungal cream (urea) can also be found in urine. Does this work?
Pierre, Ipswich

I don't know. Back in the eighties, though, I used to deal with athlete's foot by pouring cocaine on my toes. They cut the stuff with so much foot powder in those days, it was the best treatment you could find if you had an outbreak on the road, away from your local chemist's. The only problem was the price: it worked out at about three grand a toe. If I'd known about the peeing thing, I might have saved myself some cash.

Dear Dr. Ozzy:
What's the best way to get over jet-lag—quickly?
James, Toronto

They say that if you line the insides of your shoes with brown paper, it cures jet-lag. Unfortunately, like a lot of things people say, it's bollocks. In reality, there's only thing that'll stop your body clock getting messed up, and it's called staying at fucking home.

Dear Dr. Ozzy:
What's the best cure for "seasonal affective disorder"? I get incredibly depressed every year before the clocks go forward, but I can't afford to move to the Florida Keys.
Felicity, Doncaster

All you need is a bit of heat and light. If you can't afford a plane ticket, I'm not sure what to suggest, apart from setting your house on fire—which obviously ain't a very clever idea.

Dear Dr. Ozzy,

A doctor in Italy says he can cure cancer patients by giving them baking soda. What's your opinion?

Chris (no address given)

A friend of mine got cancer a few years ago and didn't want to go through any of the conventional treatments, so he spent months doing all the dead cat voodoo stuff—and now the poor bloke's dead. Obviously, I ain't gonna criticise anyone in that position, 'cos if you've been told you've only got weeks to live, you're gonna do whatever you think you need to do. But baking power? You're fixing a tumour, not a cupcake. Also, if it really worked, wouldn't baking powder be in short supply by now? Personally, my rule of thumb is that if some whacky new treatment sounds too good to be true, it is.

Dear Dr. Ozzy,

According to my great-aunt, nine white raisins, soaked in one tablespoon of gin for two weeks, will get rid of arthritis. Is this right?

Phil, Luton

The Osbourne family has the same recipe, passed down through the generations. In our version, though, there's only one white raisin, and it's soaked in nine bottles of gin, for two minutes.

It's great for pretty much anything.

DR. OZZY'S AMAZING MEDICAL MISCELLANY—

Crazy Cures Through the Ages

- In Egypt, they reckon that being buried in the sand during the hottest part of the day can cure rheumatism, joint paint, and impotence. If you stay out there long enough without water, it can also cure being alive.

- To treat a stuttering child, Chinese doctors used to recommend smacking the kid in the face—on a cloudy day. If anyone ever tried that on me, they'd get a knee in the balls, n-n-n-n-no matter what the fucking weather was.
- The only anaesthetic in Medieval England was a potion made up of lettuce juice, gall from a castrated boar, briony, opium, hemlock juice, vinegar, and what passed for wine in those days. I'm pretty sure I had exactly the same cocktail in Miami while on the road with Mötley Crüe in 1984.

Dear Dr. Ozzy:
Have you ever suffered from heartburn, or acid indigestion? If so, what do you do about it?
Joan, Shropshire

Oh, I used to get this all the time—I'd wake up at three in the morning with a horrendous burning sensation in my chest. Then one night my bed caught fire, and I realised I'd been going to sleep every night with a lit cigarette in my hand. When I stopped doing that, the problem went away.

Dear Dr. Ozzy,
Please help me—I can't stop scratching my testicles at night! It's getting so bad, my wife is threatening to sleep in another room. And now I've noticed a red rash, which seems to be spreading to my wider nether regions. Is this "jock itch"?
Ted, Northumberland

Sounds like it to me. The first thing to do is change your underwear. Personally, I find that nylon Y-fronts give me a raging case of ball itch: it's like they're on fire, man. Now, I wouldn't mention this to your missus (if you ever want her to go near you again), but it's all to do with trapped sweat. So

the next thing to do is get yourself some antifungal cream—
the same stuff you'd use for athlete's foot—and it should calm
down in a few days.

Dear Dr. Ozzy,
Thanks to your medical wisdom I already know your cure for a
cold—a Hot Ozzy—but what's the best way to **prevent one?**
Lucy, Bristol

Your local drug store will sell you any old bollocks to
"prevent" a cold—they must make a fortune out of virus
season—but the fact is, you've just gotta ride it out. There's no
harm in having a Hot Ozzy or two as a precaution, though.
If it does nothing else, it'll make your day at work go by a lot
faster.

Dear Dr. Ozzy:
What's the most effective treatment for the hiccups?
Lauren, Carlisle
Tony, New York

Extreme pain, combined with the element of surprise.

DR. OZZY'S INSANE-BUT-TRUE STORIES

The 430 Million Hiccup Man

- The longest-ever attack of hiccups went on for 68
  years—68 fucking years, man!—and was suffered by an
  American guy named Charles Osborne (no relation). It
  started in 1922, when he was weighing a hog for slaugh-
  ter in Iowa, and didn't stop until 1990. The worst thing
  is, he dropped dead from an ulcer only a year after he
  got better. The *good* news? His hiccups didn't stop him

getting on with his life: he managed to get hitched and have five kids (which proves that anyone can get laid, if they put their mind to it). He was even mentioned in *Guinness World Records* and Trivial Pursuit. Apparently, this guy hiccupped 40 times a minute in the early days, slowing down to "only" 20 times a minute as he got older. That works out at about 430 million hiccups over his entire life. It's a good job I never sat next to this guy on a plane, or I'd have pushed him out of the emergency exit after five fucking minutes.

Dear Dr. Ozzy:

What's the best cure for snoring? I need something to shut up my husband, who sounds like a whale with a foghorn stuck in its throat, before I kick him downstairs to the sofa.

Jane, Acton

I used to share a room with a guy who had the worst snore in the world, I swear. One night, I got so fed up with him, I filled up a wastepaper basket with water, put it next to his bed, and told him, "One snore, and it's going over yer head." And y'know what? It cured him. Or at least he didn't dare go to sleep until he was pretty fucking sure I'd already nodded off. Having said that, I'm a terrible snorer myself. So is Sharon. Our 17 dogs snore, too. When all of us are in action at the same time, our bedroom must sound like the London Nostril Choir. It's never bothered me, though. I'm usually asleep.

Dear Dr. Ozzy:

Is it really true that chicken soup can help with congestion?

Rita, Germany

Yes—especially if you add gasoline. Seriously though, I've definitely heard that there's a special chemical in chicken soup that breaks up all the gunk in your nose, making you breathe a bit easier...but in my experience it only lasts for as long as you're eating the stuff. It's more likely the heat of the food that gets the old snot running.

Dear Dr. Ozzy:
What's the best cure for depression?
"Peter," County Armagh

It's tempting to give you a funny response to this, but unfortunately depression ain't funny: I've suffered from it myself. What I did—and what I recommend you do—is talk to your GP. Personally, I'm on a low dose of an anti-depressant called Zoloft (also known as sertraline), and it does the job. Of course, you hear a lot of people say that anti-depressants just put a sticking plaster on the problem, instead of solving the real cause. And they might have a point...but it's very easy to say that *if you ain't fucking depressed.* The only big problem for me with anti-depressants is that they ended my sex life. Trying to get down to some action these days is like trying to raise the *Titanic.* It would be depressing if I weren't on anti-depressants. As it is, I don't give a flying one.

Dear Dr. Ozzy:
Is it true that "onion syrup"—onions cooked with brown sugar or honey—can help with a cough?
Jamie, Madrid

No idea. I *do* know that if you eat enough onions, it'll cure people from wanting to speak to you again.

Dr. Ozzy's Trivia Quiz: Magic Medicine

Find the answers—and your score—on page 263

1. Which musical instrument allegedly cures "sleep apnoea" (when you don't breathe properly at night)?
   a) A kazoo
   b) A didgeridoo
   c) An Auto-Tune machine

2. What the fuck is "Peruvian Viagra"?
   a) A squished frog
   b) A well-trained hamster
   c) A rare type of bean

3. The ancient Egyptians treated blindness with...
   a) Tickling
   b) Sunlight
   c) Bat's blood

4. Which "cure" for AIDS has actually helped spread the disease?
   a) Bonking a virgin
   b) Putting the condom on your big toe
   c) Smothering your private parts in clarified butter

5. In the 1960s, psychiatrists treated alcoholics with...
   a) Alcohol
   b) LSD
   c) Hospital-grade laxatives

CHAPTER NOTES: HOW TO CURE ANYTHING

SYMPTOM	Severe Headache	Sudden, excruciating bowel pain	Baldness	Stiff neck	Blurred vision
FIRST THING TO ASK YOURSELF	Have I been listening to NPR? *And/or...* Did I drive my car into a non-moving object?	What's the waddling distance to the nearest toilet? *And/or...* Why did I wear white trousers today?	If I shave all my hair off, will I look like Bruce Willis...or an axe murderer?	Do I have a Viagra pill stuck in my throat?	Am I underwater? *And/or...* Was the tenth pint really necessary?
QUICK FIX	Shoot the radio. *And/or...* Massage forehead with airbag.	Unclench buttocks, prepare for consequences.	Cover bare patches with spray paint. *And/or...* Wear the cat on your head.	Picture Simon Cowell in a miniskirt (should relieve any swelling).	Do what the officer says, and get out of the fountain, 'cos you're fucking busted.
WHAT NOT TO SAY TO YOUR DOCTOR LATER	"Is a brain transplant expensive?"	"D'you mind if I use your shitter? I may be some time."	"Tell me, doc: how did you feel when you turned into a slaphead?"	"When I imagined Simon Cowell in a miniskirt, my neck just got stiffer."	"I think beer gives me astigmatism."

Have a Fucking Egg

2

The Truth About Diet & Exercise

One of the saddest questions I've ever been asked as Dr. Ozzy came from a middle-aged woman in Worcester—Sally, her name was—who wanted to know if was safe to "Go to work on an egg" (as an old British ad slogan used to say). Someone had told her that yolk was bad news, so she was considering a switch to low-fat bean curds or some bullshit. I could hardly believe it, man. This woman was old enough to remember when it was considered perfectly acceptable to fry bread in lard, or let kids breathe fumes from leaded petrol. And yet she'd convinced herself that one boiled egg was gonna send her to an early grave. I mean, really? Is *that* how crazy things are now?

The trouble is, it's so easy to get things out of proportion. I'm guilty of the same thing myself. For example, I recently went through a phase of having egg-white omelettes for lunch as part of a low-calorie diet. Then one day this light blub went off in my head, and I thought to myself, "Y'know what?

This tastes like fucking shit." So I went back to eating normal omelettes, and, low and behold, I didn't grow five extra bellies overnight. As long as you're not having a dozen eggs every morning, another dozen for lunch, and another dozen for dinner, what's the problem? It the same with *anything*: all you need is a bit of common sense, and chances are, you'll be fine.*

Having said that, common sense has never exactly been one of my fortes. Because of my addictive personality, I tend to do anything and everything to excess. Like when I gave up McDonald's and switched to burritos, for example. Within 24 hours, I was addicted to the fucking burritos. Or when I gave up being a lazy-arsed bastard and started to exercise, but ended up taking a gram of speed so I could run around the block faster. It's a never-ending struggle, trying to live the perfect balanced lifestyle if you're as unbalanced as I am. As a matter of fact, I think it's hard for everyone, insane or otherwise. But as I always say to people, you should never stop trying. Just take every new day as it comes—and go easy on the triple-decker bacon chili cheeseburgers.

Dear Dr. Ozzy:
My daughter announced today that she's going on the "Five Bite Diet"—ie, she drinks what she wants (if it has no calories) but has only five bites of lunch and five bites of dinner. As a precaution, she's also taking a multi-vitamin tablet every day.
Should I try and stop her?
Julie, Sunderland

I've never heard of this before, but it doesn't surprise me that it exists. In fact, I tried a similar kind of extreme diet

---

*Before anyone gives me a bollocking, talk to a doc about your diet if you have high cholesterol.

myself once—I called it the "walking corpse" diet, 'cos even though you got thinner, it made you feel like the living dead. And of course it goes without saying that five seconds after I stopped, I put all the weight back on again. I mean, I honestly don't know what to tell you when it comes to dieting, 'cos I came to the conclusion a long time ago that nothing works apart from eating healthier and eating *less*, full stop. Catchy-sounding quick fixes are usually good for only one thing: making a shitload of dough for the person who came up with the idea. Bearing in mind that your daughter will probably do the opposite of whatever you tell her, it's at least worth getting the advice of your GP before she starts sniffing her dinner instead of eating it. That's the best way to make sure she ain't doing anything dangerous.

Dear Dr. Ozzy:
My doctor has told me that I have high cholesterol. Does that mean I should stop taking cocaine?
Andrew, Los Angeles

Hang on a fucking minute: don't you think you're putting the cart before the horse a bit here? I suppose you're thinking that because the cholesterol gives you a higher risk of a heart attack, the coke might send you over the edge. But you shouldn't be doing cocaine, full stop—never mind if you've got high cholesterol, low blood sugar, a gammy leg, or a runny nose. It's a like a forty-a-day smoker asking if he should move out of the city to get some fresh air. Where's the logic, man? Here's the thing with coke: you can drop dead from it *instantly*, 'cos you're buying it on the street, so you never know the fuck's gonna be in it. It also messes with your head, makes you say stupid things, and can land you in prison. Here's my advice: if you keep taking the coke, forget all about your cholesterol—chances are, you'll kill yourself before anything else can.

Dear Dr. Ozzy:
I can't stop drinking Coca-Cola. Do you think I've become addicted to the caffeine?
David, Staffordshire

I know plenty of people who are addicted to cola—not just the brand name stuff, but the big, cheap gallon bottles you get in a supermarket. It's not so much the caffeine you get hooked on, though: it's the *sugar*. Try switching to a diet brand. Or better yet, have a cup of tea instead.

Dear Dr. Ozzy:
My boyfriend goes swimming six times a week and does yoga twice a week, but he's still getting fat. Why?
Eve, Ireland

There's only one explanation: he's eating sandwiches between laps. Either that, or he's lying to you about the exercise. I recommend hiring a private detective to follow him around for a week. Report back.

Dear Dr. Ozzy:
Is it really true that you're a vegetarian now? Have you bitten the head off a lettuce yet?
Paul, Derby

Very funny. And yeah...I'm *borderline* vegetarian now, 'cos I find it hard to digest red meat. When I'm at home in LA, the woman who works for me—she's Ethiopian—cooks up veggies on the barbeque with brown rice. It's spicy, not boring at all, and there's nothing like a good old curry to unplug a clogged 62-year-old arsehole. Mind you, it's hard to keep it up when I'm out on the road, 'cos you can't always get hold of healthy food when you're so far away from home—although eventually you just lose your tolerance for meat, so maybe I'll have no choice. In fact, I remember one time in 1968 when one of my old bandmates from Black Sabbath, Terence

"Geezer" Butler—the first vegetarian I'd ever met—ate a hot dog in Belgium 'cos he was broke and starving, and it was the only thing he could scrounge that day. The poor bloke was in hospital a few hours later. In fact, I don't think he took another shit until 1983.

Dear Dr. Ozzy:
Is there any truth to the claim that food colouring—which used to be made out of coal-tar—makes kids hyperactive? Or is this just another one of those trendy myths?
Erica, Los Angeles

When I was growing up, no-one cared about what was in the food—calories, preservatives, colouring, or otherwise: we just ate what was on the table, 'cos the alternative was a smack round the ear and going to bed hungry. And have to say, looking back, we were all fucking *nuts*. I mean, it's hard to imagine a more hyperactive kid than I was: I spent half the day bouncing off the walls, and the other half bouncing on my bed. Was it the additives? Who knows, man. In a perfect world, we'd all grow our own food. But you can't exactly grow a fish stick or a can of beans. So my advice is just be careful and make sure that your kids are eating plenty of fruit and veggies.

DR. OZZY'S INCREDIBLY HELPFUL TIPS—

Diet—Things to Avoid

◆ If you're trying to stay slim, it ain't a good idea to take part in Nathan's Famous Hot Dog Eating Contest, held every year in New York. The last record-breaking winner scoffed 66 hot dogs—that's 19,600 calories—in 12 minutes. A few hours later, he broke another record for the amount of time he spent on the shitter.

- I've suffered the consequences of a few dodgy curries in my time, but nothing comes close to eating a badly cooked Fugu ("river pig") in Japan. The fish contains tetrodotoxin, which paralyses your muscles and stops your breathing over a period of 24 hours. There ain't no antidote, either. So if you get poisoned, it'll be the worst—and last—day of your life. It'll ruin your holiday, too.

- Fast-food has always been a guilty pleasure for me, but if there's one thing you should probably steer clear of, it's the "100×100" burger at the In-N-Out chain (you have to special order it). It comes with 100 beef patties, 100 slices of cheese, and costs about $100. That doesn't include the price of the ambulance you'll need to call after eating it.

- If you go to Sardinia on holiday, don't *ever* order Casu Marzu. It's basically a sheep's milk cheese, the difference being that it's infested with live insect larvae, which look like wriggly little white worms. I ain't fucking kidding you. The worst part is, the worms jump up and down, so you've gotta put your hand over your plate when you're eating, otherwise you end up getting 'em in your eyes and up your nose.

Dear Dr. Ozzy:
I like to drink beer, but I'm getting fat. I hate to think I might have to give up booze just to stay in shape. Is there an alternative to beer that has fewer calories?
Miles, Kailua, Hawaii

Not in Hawaii, there ain't. It's all Mai Tais, Zombies, and Hoola-tinis. There's enough fruit juice and syrup and fuck knows what else in those things to give you three extra chins in the time it takes you to drink one of 'em. The thing is, you can't have it both ways: you can't keep drinking *and* complain about getting fat. Alcohol makes you bloated, period. It's one of the most calorific substances on the planet. Having said that, if you switch to Mai Tais, you definitely won't be able to drink as *many* of them as you could beers. I mean, when I was on the booze, beers didn't even count, you could knock 'em back so easily. Some people might say, "Try pot," but then you'll get the munchies, which is twice as bad. Personally my advice would be to cut down. Or stop drinking altogether.

Dear Dr. Ozzy:
I love having a full-strength Marlboro before breakfast, but I've noticed that the first couple of drags make me want to run to the bathroom and evacuate. Is this normal?
David, Cardiff

If you're a smoker, why the fuck are you wasting time worrying about your bowels? What about your LUNGS? Having said that: yes, nicotine is a stimulant, so that world-falling-out-of-your-bottom feeling is normal. Why not stop smoking and have a glass of orange juice instead? Y'know, over the years I've taken every drug known to man, and I swear, nicotine is the worst. Take it from the Prince of Darkness: cigarettes are evil, man.

Dear Dr. Ozzy:
I noticed that you worked with a personal trainer during **The Osbournes.** *Did you find it helpful?*
James, Scarborough, Maine

Using a trainer helped me keep a routine, which is very helpful, 'cos I'm an all-or-nothing kind of guy: I'll kill myself on the treadmill one month, then spend the next one with my head in the fridge. But at the end of the day, I don't want to have to make a date in my diary to do exercise. After a while

I also got pissed off with a guy standing there in my own house, telling me, "Do another five reps." I almost punched the bastard a couple of times.

Dear Dr. Ozzy:
I've recently decided to slow down on my hedonistic lifestyle and try being healthy, so now it's all low-fat food and exercise, but when I wake up in the morning, I feel worse than I did before. How long will this last, or should I just return to my old ways?
Alex, Milton Keynes

Rome wasn't built in a day. Some people go over the top when they try to get healthy: one minute they're living a life of beer, cheeseburgers, and daytime telly, and the next they've cut out meat, alcohol, coffee, and sugar, and they're trying to run a marathon. *Of course* you're gonna feel like shit if you do that. Take it easy. One thing at a time. And if you're doing exercise, for God's sake make sure you stretch—before and afterwards.

Dear Dr. Ozzy:
What's the healthiest (and most effective) way to administer a jolt of caffeine first thing in the morning: a shot of espresso, or a full-sized mug of filter coffee?
Anonymous, Pittsburgh

I don't know about the *healthiest*, but I can tell you the *best* way—by a mile. First of all, brew yourself a normal pot of filter coffee. Then tip the coffee back into the filter and brew it again over the old grounds. At the same time, make yourself an espresso. Next step: pour yourself a cup of the double-strength filter coffee...then add the shot of espresso. I call it a "red eye": one sip, as you'll be as awake as you've even been in your life, trust me. That ain't the strongest coffee I've ever had, mind you. My old mate Frank Zappa used to make a brew that tasted like leaded gasoline. And Turkish coffee is even worse. I downed a soup bowl full of that stuff when I was in Crete once, and I spent the next three weeks jogging around the island, trying to get it to wear off.

Dear Dr. Ozzy:

Why do people say it's bad to eat chocolate before public speaking (or singing, for that matter)?

Jim, Kelso

Well, for a start, chocolate thickens your saliva, which ain't good news if you've gotta recite Shakespeare or get through "Iron Man." For me, chocolate also causes heartburn, which sends acid shooting up my esophagus, which literally burns my throat out—and that's my worst fear when I'm out on the road, 'cos it affects thousands of people when a show gets cancelled. Having said that, you're not supposed to drink tea, either, but I still do before gigs. It might not be very rock 'n' roll, but it's like a magic potion to me.

Dear Dr. Ozzy:

I know you work out a lot and have changed your lifestyle dramatically, but is it more difficult to maintain your exercise schedule and health regimen when you are touring? What do you recommend for people like me who pretty much live on the road?

John, Santa Barbara, California

To be honest with you, I don't need to go to the gym when I'm on the road: during a two-hour show, I'll burn about 2,000 calories and use muscles I don't even know I have until the next day, when I feel like I've been thrown off the Empire State Building. But here's the advice I'd give to anyone who works away from home in a sedentary job: *go for a walk.* It's one the best forms of exercise there is, and it costs nothing. The only reason I don't go for walks myself is because my arse has got a mind of its own, and if I'm out of range of a toilet, I freak out. That shouldn't stop anybody else, though.

Dear Dr. Ozzy:

I'm pretty much living on five-hour energy drinks. Is this stuff gonna hurt me in the long run?

Eric, Colorado

Well, it's not exactly food, is it? You're basically just shooting up caffeine. And if there's one golden rule I've learned over the years, it is this: what goes up, *must come down*. I remember necking a few energy drinks before going on stage once: I felt like the king of the universe for about one-and-a-half songs, but by the third number, I was ready to fucking hang myself. So if I were you, I'd try and get your energy from something that's not gonna make you drop like the *Hindenburg* when the rush wears off.

Dear Dr. Ozzy:

I'm in my mid-fifties and a stonking 350lbs. I'm addicted to food, often eating enough for three or four people. I'm out of breath, have no interest in sex, and can hardly even stand up. I'm using food like you used drugs—I'm killing myself. Any advice? Money is no object.

John, London

Number one, find a good dietician. Number two, start exercising (as long as your doc gives you the okay). But whatever you do, don't go mental. For example: start at the lowest setting on the treadmill, then work your way up *slowly*, not the other way around. The mistake I made was thinking, "Well if I turn this thing up to warp factor ten, I'll burn more calories"—but I wasn't fit enough, my legs couldn't keep up, and I almost catapulted myself backwards through a plate glass window. Another thing you have to do is find an activity you enjoy, 'cos if you don't love it, you ain't gonna do it. And I don't mean take up darts, or table football. You've gotta break a sweat. I'm 175lbs at the moment, but I could easily be 350lbs if I didn't burn off all the crap I eat with a bit of exercise. Fortunately, I've now become addicted to the blast of endorphins you get on a cross-trainer in the same way I used to be addicted to Special Brew. I've also got a massive telly in my gym at home, so while I'm getting rid of my extra chins I can watch World War II documentaries on the History Channel. That's my idea of paradise, that is—a bit of cardio and some animated battle maps.

Dear Dr. Ozzy:
I recently went to Cuba, picked up a nasty bug, and was hospitalised with dehydration. The doctors shoved a steel lozenge thing down my throat to take a biopsy from my stomach, but it didn't find the cause of the problem. Three months later, I'm still passing liquid. Please help...
Simon, Doncaster

Three months? If I was passing liquid for three *hours* I'd be straight down the gastroenterologist's, begging him to make it stop. Chances are, it was some dodgy lettuce that did it. Let me tell you something: lettuce is fucking deadly if you eat it in the wrong country. I mean, yeah, you think it's all nice and posh and healthy and whatever, but if you order a salad in parts of Mexico or South America, you might as well order a plate of raw human shit, 'cos that's what's in the water that it's been washed in. I've suffered the same fate on more than a few occasions: you cross the border to Mexico, and within a few hours, you're laid up in hospital, on a drip. But three months is no joke: it could even be more serious than you think. Best to get it checked out again.

Dear Dr. Ozzy:
I want to reduce the calories I eat, but how on earth do you go about counting them? I know that everything you buy in the supermarket has those little stickers on them now, but does anyone seriously measure out every single portion—and what about food you eat in

restaurants, or that other people cook for you? How can you keep
track of if all without basically dedicating your entire life to it?
Brian, Castle Bromwich

It's a total waste of time, counting calories. For example, I
looked at a packet of cereal the other, and it said on the side,
"one bowl, 230 calories." But how big's the bowl? For all I
know, it could be the size of an ashtray or a swimming pool. A
better strategy is just to cut your portions down. Buy smaller
plates, for a start. Seriously. Here in America, they give you
enough food in one sandwich to feed the North Korean Army
for a month. It's only when you put it on a normal-sized plate
that you realise what a pig you're being. Exercise also makes a
really big difference, even if it's just a 20-minute walk every
day. Do both of those things, and you'll never have to count
calories again.

Dear Dr. Ozzy:
What's the best way to treat a burned mouth? I love food, so there's
nothing worse than getting over-enthusiastic about a piping hot
meal, only to destroy my taste buds for a week.
Sam, Warwick

I've done that with a hot french fry before, and it's horrible.
It's even worse when you get it stuck halfway down your
wind pipe, then everything else you eat for the next month
tastes like sulphuric fucking acid. You've gotta *slow down*,
man. In England, we eat food like it could jump up and do
the 100-yard sprint at any second. Alternatively, you could eat
all your meals at a restaurant with lazy waiters, so the food's
always lukewarm.

Dear Dr. Ozzy:
Why are people so worried about the mercury in tuna fish? I read
the other day that Abraham Lincoln used to take mercury-laced

pills to treat his constipation, and he was in good enough health to
lead America (until he was shot, of course).
Percy, Cardiff

The only time I'd get worried about the mercury in tuna
fish is if I ate a whole one. Otherwise, I can't see how a bit
of sushi every now and then is a problem. Having said that,
a friend of my daughter's recently got mercury poisoning,
and it was heavy duty, man: she had memory loss, slurred
speech, crazy mood swings, loss of co-ordination...basically,
she ended up feeling how I did during most of the 1980s.
As for good old Abe Lincoln, it's never a very good idea to
say, "Oh, so-and-so survived putting leeches on his eyeballs,
so therefore it must be okay." I mean, they used to add pure
heroin to cough mixture. If they still did that today, I'd be off
sick with a cold 365 days a year.

Dear Dr. Ozzy:
People keep telling me how great yoga is—especially when it comes
to stress—but I can't stand the thought of all that chanting and
hippy-dippy bullshit. Have you ever tried it?
Sam, Beaconsfield

You've got totally the wrong idea. Doing yoga ain't like
being a Buddhist monk. Or at least it doesn't have to be. It's
basically stretching exercises—and you'd be amazed at the
results you can get. I used to have this makeup artist, and
she went on leave to have a baby, then I saw her a year later
after doing a lot of yoga, and she looked amazing, all slim and
tight and healthy. You'd *never* have believed she'd pushed one
out just a few months before. I've actually just decided to do
a course of Pilates for that very same reason. I'm not out of
shape, but I want to avoid getting a big old gut on me. My
only fear with these stretching-based things is that I won't
have the patience. Generally speaking, if I haven't worked up

a sweat in the first three seconds, I'm off. So we'll see. In the meantime, why don't you take a leaf out of my book, and at least *try* it.

DR. OZZY'S INSANE-BUT-TRUE-STORIES—

When Exercise Is Bad for You

◆ Next time you're in the gym, watch out for blokes with exploding balls—exercise balls, that is. One guy in Florida sued after the one he was leaning on (while holding two dumbbells) went pop, sending him crashing to the floor. He needed five surgeries, allegedly.

◆ No-one knew you could get high from endorphins until a guy called Jim Fixx came along in the 1970s. He was basically a fat bloke who smoked two packs a day until he started jogging—then he lost his flab, quit tobacco, and turned himself into the world's first ever fitness guru. Trouble was, he dropped dead at 52. While on a run.

◆ Scientists reckon the chance of ending up like Fixx—ie, croaking it while exercising—is roughly one in 15,000 to 18,000 every year.* People who work out the most have a higher risk than those who do it least. Being fat ain't much of an alternative, though: obesity is a far more common preventable cause of death.

◆ During the 1956 FA Cup Final, the goalie for Man City, Bert Trautmann, managed to break his neck after diving for the ball one too many times. There were still 17 minutes to go, though, so the crazy fucker kept on playing—even making a few more heroic saves that let

---

* According to *The New England Journal of Medicine*.

Man City take home the cup. In fact, the guy didn't even bother getting an X-ray until three days later, when he finally realised his head was about to fall off. He made a full recovery, and the last I heard, he's still alive and well.

Dear Dr. Ozzy:
I keep hearing that humans need to drink eight glasses of water a day. This is surely bullshit, yes?
Billy, Leicester

I tried drinking eight classes of water a day for a while, and my bladder felt like a red-hot fucking cannon ball. I need to pee a lot as it is—but if I'm knocking back eight glasses of water, I might as well just live in the can, the amount of time I'll end up spending in there. My advice is this: if you eat a lot of fruit and vegetables, you'll get some water from your food. On the top of that, drink as much as you need to stop being thirsty—which means if you lose water from exercise, you'll be thirstier, and need to drink a bit more. That's what animals do to survive when they're in the wild. We ain't any different.

Dear Dr. Ozzy:
I've become addicted to counting calories: I have a sensor in my shoes that sends a "calorie burn readout" to my iPhone; I input everything I eat into a calorie counting website; and I try to estimate how many calories I burn up doing everything else (including typing this). I'm losing weight, but going insane. Advice?
William, Berkshire

I remember seeing an interview with Bob Dylan after he wrote his memoirs, and he said, "While you're writing, you ain't living." The same goes for counting calories—which I've tried to do on many occasions. The bottom line is, every hour you spend jotting down every last cornflake or baked bean you ate during the day is an hour you could have spent with your family or friends. Either that, or you could be using the time to *learn* something, like a new language. I mean, okay, yeah, you'd still be fat. But at least you'd be fat and able to order your double-cheeseburgers in Slovakian.

Dear Dr. Ozzy:
I haven't been able to "go" for ten days, and I'm starting to get really worried. Nothing seems able to unclog me.
Barry, Aberdeen

I'd recommend a strong cup of coffee, but it sounds more like you need a stick of dynamite. Prunes can also be effective, if you can stand the taste. Personally, if I'm suffering from a spot of constipation, I'll ask the missus for some of her "special pills." All women seem to have a stash of these things somewhere: they come in a pink box with flowers on the outside. Just be careful: I once took a handful of 'em, thinking they'd never work—nothing else did—but boy, was I wrong. Two minutes later, I was unloading about ten Christmas dinners out of my rear end. It went on for *days*, to the point I couldn't even work out where all the stuff was coming from. It was like the laws of physics didn't apply. So I suggest trying to get hold of the same stuff. Just go easy with it.

Dear Dr. Ozzy,
I love lattes, but just one medium cup gives me a headache and makes my heart race. Is this normal?
Anne, Tyneside

I learned the answer to this question when I got my DNA downloaded onto a computer chip in 2010: we all metabolise caffeine at different speeds, based on the way our genes work. Personally, I feel like my head's about to blast off to Mars after one sip of espresso, and now I know why: my body can't process it. It sounds as though you're built the same way. Unfortunately, there's only one thing you can do: switch to another drink. Trying to beat your own genes is a game you're only ever gonna lose.

Dear Dr. Ozzy:
How much vitamin C is healthy? I'm taking 4,000mgs a day in the hope of avoiding a cold.
Meredith, Surrey

I might be wrong, but I'm pretty sure your body can only store so much vitamin C: the rest just passes right through you. So even if you take 5 million units or whatever, it won't do much good. The sad fact is, if you're gonna get the flu... you're gonna get the flu.

Dear Dr. Ozzy,
Every time I drink milk I get the most horrific eggy flatulence you've ever had the misfortune to smell. I can clear out entire restaurants with it. Does this mean I'm "lactose intolerant," or is that just some bullshit that Hollywood-types have invented?
Glen, London

It ain't bullshit. I've got a friend who literally turns green when she drinks milk. Try switching to soy milk for a week, then wait 'til a good old rumbler comes down the pipe, and let it loose in a confined area. If everyone's still conscious after five minutes, problem solved.

Dear Dr. Ozzy,
During important meetings, my stomach growls loud enough for everyone in the room to hear. It happens even after I've eaten a good breakfast. Please help—it's terribly awkward.
Terry, Belfast

Nerves. I guarantee it. It might even be a symptom of IBS (irritable bowel syndrome). At least you're not breaking wind, though: that's *really* embarrassing. Trust me. Especially when it sends a stale breeze through the room. That's the thing with the human brain: when it's stressed out, it'll find all kinds of ways to mess with you, from making you feel like you need to pee all the time, to bringing you out in a rash. Which is horrible, really, 'cos those are the kind of things that just make the original problem worse. The good news is that there are all kinds of potions you can take to help calm you down, including a special kind of beta blocker, which they use for stage fright.

Ask your GP about it.

Dear Dr. Ozzy:
I've joined a cycling club to get fit, and a lot of my fellow members— all men—have told me that I should shave my legs to become "more aerodynamic." Isn't this a bit weird? I mean, how much more aerodynamic can you possibly get by removing a few leg hairs?
Jim, Exeter

Unless they start asking you to wear ladies' knickers, I wouldn't worry about it. Also, from what I understand, the shaving ain't just about aerodynamics—it also makes it a lot easier to treat an injury on your leg if you fall off, which happens a lot if you compete in heavy-duty road races.

Dear Dr. Ozzy:
Whenever I eat, or have a "number two," my nose runs continually. I'm not joking—it's driving me bananas. What can I do about this (other than buying shares in Kleenex)?
Jacky (No address given)
PS: I'm not allergic to anything that I know of.

All kinds of crazy things can make your nose run because of the way your ears, nose and throat are all linked together. Personally, I get bunged up all the time 'cos of everything from dust mites to dodgy smells, so you might want to investigate allergies a bit more. Washing out your sinuses regularly with saline spray might help, although if you do it wrong, it feels like you're being fucking waterboarded. You could also be reacting to the temperature of the food you're eating, or how spicy it is. I mean, if ate a lamb vindaloo every day, my nose would run, too. Again, nasal sprays might help. So might antihistamines, if your doc approves. As for the "number twos"—that's pretty far-out, man. Maybe the sensation of pushing is triggering the same thing as the food? Ask your GP if he can send you to an ear, nose, and throat guy for a consultation.

Dear Dr. Ozzy:
Every so often, I get these nasty little bumps on my tongue which ruin my sense of taste. Please help.
Saeed, Leeds

By the sound of your question, this has happened to you a number times, and the bump has come and gone without making your tongue fall out or your head explode. So why are you worrying? Having said that, if it were me and something weird puffed up somewhere, I'd be straight down the doc to get it checked out. Given that you've gone to the trouble of writing in, it's obviously bothering you, so you should do the same.

Dear Dr. Ozzy:
Is it true that eating a big meal late at night makes you fatter than if you ate the same meal for lunch?
Dolly, Hereford

It depends. I mean, if you're a competitive eater who can shove 98 cream pies down her throat in four minutes, then I somehow don't think you'd put on less weight if you ate 'em for breakfast instead of dinner. On the other hand, if you have a normal diet, it seems logical that it's better to eat as early as you can—not only so your body has a chance to metabolise, but also to prevent acid reflux syndrome. The trouble is, if I don't have a good meal at night, I can't sleep, especially after a two-hour gig. So I'll end up having a salad, then five minutes later, ordering a pizza. That's why I've gotta watch myself on the road, 'cos I wanna be the Prince of Darkness, not the Prince of Fatness.

Dear Dr. Ozzy:

My husband wants to take me to a sushi restaurant for the first time. Aside from radiation fears (the fish isn't from Japan), is there anything I should avoid for health reasons, or is all the stuff I've heard about the danger of raw fish overblown?

Zara, Durham

The thing to remember about sushi—Western-style sushi, anyway—is that it ain't like the smelly old haddock you used to get from the fishmonger when you were little. From what I understand, sushi-grade fish is bled, gutted and packed in ice very, very quickly—and is usually frozen long enough to kill any of the parasites that might cause you any problems. Having said that, I'd avoid Fugu ("river pig") if it's on the menu (see page 22).

Dear Dr. Ozzy:

I need to lose weight fast for a wedding—are diet pills a good idea?

Ben, Stevenage

Up to you—as long as you bear in mind that some of those pills come with pretty weird-sounding side-effects, like "gas with oily spotting." You don't want to break wind during the best man's speech and feel like the Deepwater Horizon just sprang a leak in your underwear.

Dear Dr. Ozzy:

I've just read about an 82-year-old man in India—his name is Prahlad Jani—who claims not to have eaten a single thing since 1942, because he draws nourishment from meditation. (He hasn't

drank anything, either, allegedly.) Could this be possible, given that the longest-ever hunger strike went on for just 74 days?
Derek, Peebles

I don't know, but I'm gonna get my assistant on the phone ASAP and send this guy a curry—he must be *starving*. Actually, the whole thing seems pretty fishy to me. I mean, there's no way I could meditate or go without a hot dinner for that long. I'm ready to throw a brick at someone after sitting cross-legged for 69 seconds, never mind 69 years.

Dr. Ozzy's Trivia Quiz: Health Nut

Find the answers—and your score—on page 263

1. If you ate one tablespoon each of these foods, which would slam you with the most calories?
   a) Goose fat
   b) Ghee (clarified butter, used in curries)
   c) Unsalted butter

2. Farting less often is easy if you...
   a) Swallow less air
   b) Drink more water
   c) Cut down on beans, sugar-free chewing gum...and pears

3. Speaking of unwanted trouser explosions...how many times does the average person let rip every day?
   a) 14 times (1–4 pints of gas)
   b) Twice (half a pint of gas)
   c) 27 times (8–12 pints of gas)

4. What causes "heavy leg syndrome"?
   a) Involvement with the Mafia
   b) Exercising too much
   c) Not enough blood circulation

5. How old was the fitness guru/muscleman Jack LaLanne when he died?
   a) 41
   b) 96
   c) 73

CHAPTER NOTES: FITNESS METHODS

TYPE OF EXERCISE	Running	Swimming	Cycling	Weight-Lifting	Yoga
HANDY TIP	Start your workout close to something that might kill you. You'll run faster.	Some holiday resorts have bars in their pools.	If you like cross-dressing, this is the best excuse you'll ever get for shaving your legs.	You can get paid to do this.... by becoming a professional bag carrier.	Find the best-looking woman in the class and stand behind her. It'll cheer you up to no end.
DANGERS & ANNOYANCES	The thing that might kill you...might kill you. Also beware of ball chafing, heart attacks.	Some pools with bars have yellow fucking water. Also beware of sharks, rip-tides, overly tight swim trunks.	Saying, "But darling, it's for aerodynamic reasons" ain't gonna fly if you're also wearing fishnets and a bra.	Looking like a weight-lifter.	Bulges can be spotted easily through Lycra.
PAY-OFF	Feeling healthy 'cos you're wearing a track suit.	When you get tired, you can always float.	Putting on silk stockings without them ripping.	Looking like a weight-lifter.	Being able to jump off a drum riser while doing the splits—and not wake up in hospital.

Pruning

3

Cleanliness Is Next to Ozzyness

When I was growing up in Aston, my idea of a personal grooming was a hot bath every other year. It's not like there was a lot of pressure to be smooth-skinned and beautiful in those days. As a bloke, you were hairy and smelly, full stop, end of story. And as a bloke who was also a rock 'n' roll singer, you were basically a one-man walking fucking sewer. I went on tour in Scandinavia once—in the depths of winter—with only one change of underpants. And no toothpaste. By the time I got back on the ferry to Harwich, Essex, my breath was so bad, every time I opened my mouth to say something, flowers wilted and birds fell out of the sky.

I'm a new man now.

The first time I really experienced modern beauty treatments was when I met Sharon. I woke up one day and she had me in a headlock with a pair of tweezers in her hand. I remember screaming, *"What the fuck you DOING?!"* She just tightened her grip and went, "I'm giving you a long-overdue pruning, Ozzy, that's what I'm fucking doing."

That's what Sharon calls it: "pruning." And she does it to me at every available opportunity. If she sees so much as a single nose hair—she calls 'em "Hitlers" 'cos they look like the Führer's moustache—she'll go after it like a lioness going after her prey. After a while I gave up trying to escape, 'cos putting up a fight wasn't worth the pain. By holding out, I was making only one person miserable: *me*. Besides, I didn't exactly want to go around looking like three different families of crows had set up a nest in my conk.

It's reached the point these days where I actually enjoy a pruning—especially if it involves a long massage before a gig. I might be the Prince of Darkness, but I've had more pedicures now than I've had hot dinners. I don't take it too far, though. I've never had my balls waxed. My anus has never been bleached. And I ain't into all that "caviar facial" bollocks.

To me, looking good is about working with what you've got, and taking care of the simple things. Then again, if something really, *really* bothers you, I ain't got any bones about saying, "Get it fixed." Going under the knife once in a while doesn't mean you automatically end up like Michael Jackson or that crazy Cat Woman in New York. You've just gotta make sure you save up enough dough to pay for a top-notch doctor—and you've gotta know when enough's enough. In the meantime, you'll be amazed what you can achieve with a bit of regular maintenance.

———

Dear Dr. Ozzy:
I'm a 24-year-old single man with a big date coming up, and I want to make sure I look good in the buff—y'know, just in case. With that in mind: should I trim my armpit hair?
Simon, Bethnal Green, London

How long can your armpit hair possibly be, man? I mean, I could understand if you were worried about the hair on your head, or the smell of your cologne, or what kind of clothes you're gonna wear—but unless you're planning to get this poor woman in a nude headlock over dinner, how the fuck do your armpits come into the equation? Since you asked, though, let me give you some man-to-man advice: I shaved my armpits once for a joke, and it hurt like you wouldn't believe for a whole month. Worse than that, they broke out in an 'orrible pimply rash. So if I were you, I'd leave your armpits well alone and concentrate on something else, like your conversation skills.

Dear Dr. Ozzy,

I can't resist the temptation to squeeze my blackheads and spots, even though I know I'm not supposed to. Is this bad? Does anyone seriously just wait until they "pop" by themselves?

Chris, Kent

None of my spots ever go unsqueezed because of Sharon: if she sees one, she'll be at it with a hammer and chisel in a heartbeat. You're right, though: you're not supposed to start hacking away at your forehead, or you'll leave behind a scar, give yourself an infection, or force that white gunky stuff in the wrong direction, making you look like Elephant Man. If you've got a bit of dough in the bank, go and see a good facialist and they'll do the squeezing for you. Pressing a hot towel to your face and then massaging the pores can also help. Whatever you do, make sure you wash your hands thoroughly first.

Dear Dr. Ozzy,

My ears stick out at right angles. I wouldn't mind if they did something more useful—like picking up Sky Sports—but they just make me look like an idiot. What should I do?

Neil, Glasgow

No-one wants to walk around the place looking like the Ryder Cup. But I think you're being a bit hard on your poor old lugs—the job of hearing is pretty important (take it from someone who's half-deaf). And Prince Charles does alright with his ears, which he could rent out at the weekend as parasails. But my advice is always the same with these things: if it bothers you, *do something about it.* Yes, the operation might be expensive. But buying an iPad or a new telly is also expensive, and no-one ever seems to have any problem saving up dough for that. If your ears are making you miserable enough to write to Dr. Ozzy, it might be the best investment you ever make.

Dear Dr. Ozzy:
I'm in my mid-thirties and sadly losing my hair. Should I resign myself to my fate, or fight it by any means necessary? How do you maintain your manly flowing locks?
Leo, Maryland

I've always been blessed with good hair. I don't wear a rug. I don't wear extensions. And I don't use spray paint to touch-up bald spots. The only thing I do to my hair is dye it. In fact, I've always promised myself that if I ever start getting threadbare on top, I'll shave it all off rather than getting an Irish (Irish jig = wig) or spending half the day trying to arrange my last three strands into a greasy comb-over. I mean, whenever I see these guys with crazy rugs, or the ones who wear cowboy hats all the time, I just wanna say to them, "Fuck off, we all know you ain't got any hair." And while it's possible to buy some very good wigs these days if you've got the time, the dough, and the patience, most of 'em are ludicrous. I remember one time, I sat down at a bar in New York next to a bloke with the worst wig I'd seen in my life. It was ginger, and made him look like a cat had died on his head...I mean, buying a wig is one thing. But a *ginger* one? In the end I reached up, pulled it off, and used it to mop up my spilled beer. The guy went fucking mental. But if it taught him to be bald and proud, I did him a favour.

DR. OZZY'S AMAZING MEDICAL MISCELLANY—

Beauty Secrets Through the Ages

- If you've got bad skin, try using a three-inch-deep layer of white powder foundation to cover it. Then add some smudged eye-liner and fake blood. It won't get you laid, but it'll get you out of babysitting duties for the rest of your life.
- They say that putting a cold tea bag on a bruise will make it go away faster. If a doctor ever asks if you're up for a bit of "tea-bagging," though, it's best to say "no." He might mean something else.
- If a bird craps on your head while you're standing under a tree, wave and say thanks—in Japan, that's considered a $150-a-pop facial treatment. (The stuff they use is a powder made from nightingale shit.)
- In the Philippines, mothers have been known to cut their baby's eyelashes 'cos they think it makes them grow back longer and darker when they're older. Personally, I wouldn't trust anyone to hold a pair of sharp scissors anywhere near a baby's eyeballs. The kid ain't gonna thank you for his long eyelashes if he needs a white fucking stick to cross the road.
- If you think rinsing your mouth out with Listerine tastes bad, you should have been around in Ancient Roman times: in those days, dental hygiene meant gargling with piss (as long as it came from someone Portuguese).

Dear Dr. Ozzy:

I'm thinking of getting some cosmetic surgery done, but I feel very self-conscious about anyone seeing me with bandages over my face during the recovery period—and I'm also concerned about the stares I'm going to get when I show up in the office with a completely different face. What's the best way to handle all this?
Sarah, Keswick

What exactly are you planning to do when your face is all bandaged up—go clubbing for a week in Cancun? The fact is, you're gonna have to stay indoors and rest after the operation, so you won't need to see *anyone* unless you want to. Over in California, they put you up in a special hotel where there's a whole floor for recovering patients. If it's a cheapo job, then obviously you ain't gonna get that kind of service, but in that case I'd recommend that you wait until you can afford a better surgeon. As for the last part of your question: I don't understand why you're changing your appearance in the first place if you're worried about people *noticing* your change of appearance. It sounds to me like you haven't thought this through. If I were you, I'd put everything on hold until you've had a long talk with a therapist and sorted this out in your head.

Dear Dr. Ozzy,

I'm a man of very limited stature (5ft). Should I buy platform shoes, or will that make me look sillier?
Gary, Belfast

Depends on the shoes. I ain't short, but I used to wear these silver, glittery platform things in the 1970s, and I thought they looked the dog's bollocks. Mind you, I was doing a lot of acid at the time. My advice to you is not to worry so much about what other people think. If you don't mind being short, be short. And if you want to look like you're in ABBA, go for it.

Dear Dr. Ozzy:

How can I get my skin to be as flawless as yours?

Nora, Dublin, Ireland

All I do is use a good natural cream—nothing fancy, not the two-grand-a-bottle bullshit—every morning and every night. What you've got to remember is that your face is out in the elements all the time, which means it has to deal with sun, dust, grime, and all other kinds of other crap. Also, as skin ages, it gets drier, so you need to blast it with as much moisture as possible. Personally I don't bother with facials, unless Sharon has someone over the house and ropes me into it. She's got skin creams up the fucking yin-yang—which I suppose is alright if you're a woman. But speaking as the owner of a pair of testicles, I like to keep my daily grooming time down to the bare minimum.

Dear Dr. Ozzy:

I was looking at some holiday pictures recently and realised—with horror—that I have a quadruple chin. I look like a cross between my grandma and a concertina. Help!

John, Hastings

I used to have more chins than a Chinese phone book. It's a genetic thing with my family—we all have this balloon of fat under our jaws. When I complained to my GP about it, he told me to grow a beard, but I didn't want a beard. So in the end I fixed it with liposuction. They stick a needle into the blubber, suck it out, and send you away with a bandage around your face, like you've just had the worst dentist's appointment of your life. Luckily, I didn't notice the pain, 'cos I was still blasted all the time in those days. It's like I always say, if something bothers you every time you look in the mirror, and if the technology exists to sort it out—and you've got the dough—then do it.

It changed my life.

Dear Dr. Ozzy,

Plucking my eyebrows makes me sneeze—why do you think this is, and how can I stop it happening?

Louise, Essex

I have exactly the same problem. Putting on eye make-up before a gig always sends the snot flying in all directions—my green room is *literally* a green room. The reason it happens (so I believe) is your sinuses, which go all the way up your face to your eyebrow area. When you pluck your eyebrows you're basically tickling them. The bad news is that the only way to stop it happening is to stop plucking. So you either have to put up with the occasional sneezing fit, or get ready to start looking like a walking hedgerow.

Dear Dr. Ozzy,

I was born with a pale complexion but would love to get a suntan—people with brown skin look so much healthier. What the best way to do this without resorting to tin foil?

Vicky, Sunderland

Whatever you do, don't go to an old-fashioned tanning salon. I went to one of those joints once, turned the machine straight up to level ten-and-a-half, and passed out on the bed. Then I woke up a few hours later looking like I'd been hit by an atomic bomb. I was furious with myself for months, 'cos I could hardly walk—never mind smile, or bend over, or do anything that involved creasing even the tiniest part of my skin. I might as well have paid someone to throw me in a bath of acid, it probably would have been less painful. It ages you by decades, too. A few doses of the hard stuff and you'll end up with a face like an 18th century football. I urge you to avoid anything to do with UV rays—far too dangerous for my liking—and get one of those quickie spray-on jobs instead. It won't last long, and you might smell a bit funny the day after, but it won't give you third-degree burns and it won't give you cancer, which is enough for me.

Dear Dr. Ozzy:
What's the best way to get rid of warts?
Tim, Dartmouth
  Antifreeze and fire. I don't recommend it, though.

Dear Dr. Ozzy:
I'm in my mid-40s and stunned to find that my hair is turning white (not the hair on my head). I thought I could use dye, but some hairs are black and I don't want to look like a tabby. It's getting me down and is threatening to affect my love life, which I was hoping to ignite with the local plastic surgeon before it's too late. Help!
Katy, Buckinghamshire
  Personally, I've never had a bikini wax, and I don't know why any bloke in his right mind would ever let another bloke anywhere near his nearest and dearest. For women, though, it's a lot more common—and in your case, it sounds like the lawnmower treatment might not be a bad idea. Just don't get carried away. Over in LA, some women get this thing done called "revirgination" (where they repair your hymen) while gay blokes are getting parts of their bodies bleached that should never even see the light of day. I wouldn't recommend any of that. But a bit of hot wax might do the trick.

Dear Dr. Ozzy:
I recently lost a lot of weight and now I have horrendous stretch marks. How can I get rid of them?
Michael, Kent
  This is the problem with losing weight as you get older: all the elasticity in your skin disappears, so you end up with a big,

floppy bag of skin hanging over your arse. Either that, or you get the dreaded stretch marks. I've got to ask you a question, though, Michael: *where* are these marks? If they're under your clothes, why do anything? Who cares? Otherwise, have a look on the Internet for all the oils and potions you can put on your skin to help get rid of the redness, or ask your doc about laser treatment. Getting yourself zapped can be very pricey, but I'm told it can be very effective.

Dear Dr. Ozzy:

I'm desperate to get some tattoos, but I'm broke, and my parents won't help me out, because they don't approve. Can I do them myself with a needle and some ink, like you did?
Jason, Cardiff

Yes, you can do it yourself, but I strongly advise you not to, 'cos all kinds of things can go wrong if you start stabbing yerself with a rusty fork. Either that, or you need to become a qualified tattoo artist. Personally, I learned while I was doing time for burglary in Winson Green prison, Birmingham: anything to make the day go by quicker. I remember one of the guys drawing a picture of The Saint on my arm with a ballpoint pen—I'd been a fan of the show since it started in 1962—then he used a sewing pin he'd nicked from the workroom and some melted grate polish (the stuff they used to clean fireplaces with) to poke in a tattoo over the top. After that, I was hooked. I once spent a whole afternoon in Sutton Park, a posh part of town, spelling out "O-Z-Z-Y" across my knuckles. Then I put a smiley face on each of my knees to cheer myself up when I was sitting on the bog in the morning. My old man wasn't very fucking impressed, mind you. He took one look at me, shook his head, and went, "Son, you're an *idiot*."

Dr. Ozzy's Trivia Quiz: Being Beautiful

Find the answers—and your score—on page 263

1. What crazy beauty secret did Cleopatra use to always look good?
   a) Smearing crocodile shit on her face
   b) Putting ass's milk up her ass
   c) Banning mirrors in her house

2. Which of these unlikely ingredients have been found in baldness cures throughout history?
   a) Burnt mice
   b) Ground horse teeth
   c) "Bear grease" (whatever the fuck that is)

3. If you sit for a long time behind a car window on a sunny day, what's most likely to happen?
   a) You'll tan faster than The Situation
   b) You won't turn brown, but you'll burn like Guy Fawkes on November 5
   c) You won't tan or burn—but people will start mistaking you for Yoda

4. Who spent $24,000 (more or less) on a single haircut in 2009?
   a) Tony Blair
   b) Michael Jackson
   c) The Sultan of Brunei

5. What do the Czechs bathe in before and/or after drinking beer?
   a) Beer
   b) Horse sweat
   c) Sausage fat

Family—The *Other* F-Word

4

You Love 'Em to Death,
but They Drive You Fucking Mental

Last December, my wife had one of her brilliant ideas. "Ozzy," she said to me one morning. "Let's go to England, get all the kids together, and have a traditional family Christmas in our family home in the English Countryside. It'll be lovely. What do you think?"

"Are you *sure*?" I said. "The kids are grown-up now. Maybe they want to do their own thing."

"Oh, Ozzy," she said. "*Of course* they'll want to be with their mum and dad. Besides, it's the house where they all grew up."

I wasn't very convinced. "Look, Sharon," I said. "Are you *absolutely* sure you know what you're doing?"

"Of course I do!" she replied.

Needless to say, it was a fucking disaster. Peace on earth? It would have been more peaceful if we'd gone to Tripoli. Could the kids get along with each other for more than five seconds? *Not on your life.* If it wasn't one, it was the other. All I could hear were slammed doors, houseplants being thrown across the room, and people screaming at each other. It was so bad at one point, I almost fell off the wagon and had a beer. Finally, on Christmas day, I got up, went downstairs, and said to everyone, "Look: all I want for Christmas is for you to get on, even if you have to fake it—*just for ONE fucking day!*"

Everyone nodded, hung their heads, and agreed to calm down. It lasted three hours. Then they were back at it again, worse than before. It broke my heart, to be honest with you— and it broke Sharon's heart, too. I was just so disappointed, y'know? But you can only do so much with your kids, then you've just got to let 'em get on with it. The thing is, everyone wants the perfect family—but it doesn't exist. We all dream of our cozy little domestic get-togethers, where everyone says how much they love each other, everyone remembers the good times, and no-one gets angry or jealous or has any issues. As Dr. Ozzy, I've come to realise that all families are made up of human beings, and human beings are by their very nature messy and emotional and full of all kinds of fears and insecurities. If that sounds familiar to you, I recommend you read on, 'cos this chapter takes you through just about every issue you're ever likely to face with your own flesh and blood, all the way from the womb to the nursing home.

I: BASIC PARENTING

Dear Dr. Ozzy:
My husband and I are trying to have a second baby, and we'd love it to be a girl. Is there anything we can do in the bedroom department to skew the odds in our favour?
Pamela, London

I've heard lots of whacky theories about "gender swaying" over the years: do it standing on your head for a boy; keep your left sock on for a girl; drink lemon juice for a boy; cranberry juice for a girl...etc., etc. It's all bollocks if you ask me, and the bottom line is, even if you want a girl and you get a boy, you ain't gonna love him any less. And there's something to be said for the surprise. When Sharon and I had our son, Jack, we had no idea what sex he was, 'cos he was lying in a funny position when they did the sonogram. In fact, we were convinced he was gonna be a girl, 'cos we had two daughters already, so when he popped out with a full set of tackle, our jaws hit the floor. If you want more certainty, a fertility clinic might be able to help—you can probably order a kid with purple hair and glow-in-the-dark eyes, never mind a girl—but if I were you, I'd stop worrying. The only thing that *really* matters is that your little one is healthy.

Dear Dr. Ozzy:

My wife's pregnant, and every time we leave the house, I get paranoid that her "waters" might break. What does this **mean,** *anyway? Would I have to deliver the baby myself?*

Jason, Cardiff

From what I understand—which ain't very much—babies grow inside a little watery sac thing, and when that bursts, the kid's ready to pop out. That's what it means when a pregnant woman's "water breaks." But there's no need to get all paranoid about it: even if it happens in public, it doesn't mean you have to deliver your son with a toilet plunger and wooden spoon, or whatever it is you're imagining. All you need to do is drive your missus to the nearest hospital, sharpish. In fact, that's exactly what I had to do when my first daughter, Jessica, was born. The only problem was, I didn't know how to drive, and I'd been drinking all day. Apart from that, it was easy.

Dear Dr. Ozzy:

My three-year-old son keeps being hit/kicked/bitten by the son of one of my friends. Worse, my friend never does anything about it. What can I do?

Catherine, Washington, UK

As a parent, you've just gotta accept that some kids play rougher than others. That's all very well to say, mind you, until some brat whacks your little pumpkin over the back of the head with a wooden hammer. That happened to one of my own kids at a playground in Staffordshire once, and before I even had time to think, I just turned around and chinned the other kid's dad. Looking back, I should have said something when the bullying first started—but I let it continue, getting worse and worse, until I finally blew my top. So I recommend you talk to your friend now—before she ain't your friend any more.

Dear Dr. Ozzy:

Is it true that a cat might try to suffocate a newborn baby? My husband and I have just had our first child, and need to know if we should get rid of our eight-year-old moggy.

Victoria, Isle of Wight

I used to worry about the same thing. Basically, cats like sleeping in warm places—which is why they jump into cots—and people say they can smell the milk on a baby's breath. But you don't need to frog-march poor old Mr. Moggins outside at dawn and shoot him. Just keep the door to your baby's room closed (as long as you've got a monitor) when the little one's alseep. Problem solved.

DR. OZZY'S INCREDIBLY HELPFUL TIPS—

Operating Instructions for Children

◆ Remember, babies aren't that much different from rock stars. They go crazy if they don't get enough to drink.

They feel a lot better after they've thrown up on your new carpet. And they crap their pants more than once a day. Basically, the same as me during the most of the eighties.

◆ Most strollers nowadays come with a beer holder and an ashtray. In an emergency, they can be also used to carry milk bottles and wet wipes.

◆ Don't even *think* about asking your own parents for advice about raising infants. At the age of 62, I'm lucky if I can remember why I just walked into a room, never mind how I changed a fucking nappy in 1972. Mind you, I don't think I ever *did* change a nappy, so even if I could somehow go back in time, I still wouldn't have a clue. Work out it for yourself.

Dear Dr. Ozzy:
I taught my three-year-old son a swear word for a laugh and now I can't get him to stop saying it. I'm mortified. What should I do?
Catherine, Aberdeen

Never, *ever*, swear in front of little kids: their brains are hard-wired to pick up it—trust me. You can't get 'em to learn the alphabet to save your life, but they'll memorise every filthy word in the Oxford English dictionary in a heartbeat. I mean, yeah, it might crack you up to hear a toddler effing and blinding, but ain't so funny when you take your little blue-eyed angel to the in-laws', and he goes, "Hello grandma, you c***."

Dear Dr. Ozzy:
My wife has signed up our son for football practice, piano lessons, and yoga. He's two. Is this insane?
Alex, Oxford

It sounds like he's ready to become Prime Minister. I mean, how old is David Cameron—four-and-a-half? Seriously though, my advice would be to leave the kid alone. Buy him a cowboy suit. Get him a fucking Lego set. It's your missus who should sign up for something—like therapy. A lot of parents these days just seem to be passing on all their insecurities onto their kids. I mean, piano lessons at two? Give me a break, man. What's next? Pilot training and deep sea diving classes? We pile all this pressure on to these little people then wonder why they're burned out at nine. My advice: *slow down.*

Dear Dr. Ozzy:
My four-year-old daughter is addicted to Angry Birds on my iPad. Will this cause her any harm?
Scott, Los Angeles

I don't understand a single word of this question. Why do you have birds on your iPad, and why are they pissed off? The only thing I can think of is that this is some kind of video game. If so, I don't think there's anything wrong with your daughter playing it—it's probably good for her—as long as there's a time limit. And instead of snatching it away when her fifteen minutes (or whatever) is up—which will just make her want it more—trying distracting her with something else instead...like ice cream, *heh-heh-heh.*

Dear Dr. Ozzy:
Did you think twice before vaccinating your kids, given the controversey over vaccines and autism, or do you think the fear is overblown by a few hysterical Hollywood actor types?
Steve, Bognor

Hand on heart, I can't say I had anything to do with the decision to vaccinate our kids—I was too busy vaccinating *myself* with lakes of booze. But I was as freaked out as the next parent when I heard all the talk a few years ago about the shots being linked to autism (the research turned out to be bullshit, but a lot of people are still very concerned). I mean, my sister got the flu vaccine this winter, and then came down with the worst flu of her life. So in a way it seems to make sense. But the thing is, they don't stick needles in kids for fun—they do it 'cos the diseases they prevent are fucking horrendous. The only reason we don't realise how bad things like whooping cough are is because they've been wiped out by the drugs. But here in California, where I live, babies are now dying from it again, 'cos no-one's getting their shots. To me, it doesn't make sense to expose your kids to things you *know* are dangerous to avoid something that hasn't been proved to be dangerous—no matter how suspicious you might be of vaccine companies and their dodgy motives. But everyone's different, and at the end of the day, it's a decision you have to make for yourself.

Dear Dr. Ozzy,
I'm about to become the father of a baby boy, and while I'm not Jewish, I'm wondering if I should get him circumcised—it just seems so much cleaner. What's your opinion?
Alan, Leicester

I ain't Jewish, either, but I still got the old rusty scissor treatment—even though my two younger brothers didn't. I remember asking my mum what she was thinking, expecting some kind of logical explanation. Instead, she just went, "Oh, it was the fashion." The *fashion*? This was my most prized possession she was talking about, not a pair of bell-bottom jeans! Luckily I didn't get any stick for the way I looked in the showers at school, mainly 'cos in those days, the only showers we got were when it rained. But is it more hygenic? Well, given some of the very dark and smelly places I explored in the 1970s, I would say "yes." For most people, though, a bar of soap is probably just as effective.

Dear Dr. Ozzy:

Ever since our baby daughter was born, our three-year-old son has started to regress—making goo-goo, gah-gah noises, etc. Should we tell him to grow up and act like a "big boy," or go along with it while making sure to give him more special attention?

Martha, Brixton

I feel very sad for the poor kid, 'cos he probably thinks his mum and dad don't love him as much, now there's a brand-new sibling in the house. As one of six Osbourne kids, I can fully sympathize. Because your son's feeling insecure, I wouldn't get mad at him for making the baby noises. That could just make it worse. A better idea would be to make an extra special effort to give him some one-on-one attention: buy him an ice cream, take him to his favourite park...whatever. You just need to reassure him that he ain't forgotten. If he keeps making the baby noises after that, don't tell him to stop it, just ask him gently to use his "big boy voice." My guess is he'll grow out of it before long.

Dear Dr. Ozzy:

My wife wants to give our baby a pacifier. I'm putting up a fight, because I think it'll be an impossible habit to break. What's your expert medical opinion on this matter?

David, Cornwall

If you're looking for some moral support, you've come to the wrong guy. I once sent a private jet halfway across America to go and get "Baby"—my son Jack's teddy bear—after we left it in a hotel room. That fucking teddy bear pretty much ended up with its own security detail, we were so scared of losing it. We've still got it today, in fact. Meanwhile, my daughter Kelly didn't just have one pacifier, she had two: one for each finger. And if it's any reassurance, breaking the habit wasn't difficult at all: one day, she just got bored of it, like kids do. Then it was straight on to the next big, exciting thing: her thumb.

Dear Dr. Ozzy:

I was looking through my 3-year-old son's locker at nursey school the other day and discovered that his best male friend—same age— sent him a Valentine's Day card. What's more: the boy in question has two gay dads. I know we're supposed to be cool about this kind of thing nowadays, but I'm freaking out. Advice?
Eric, Derby

It sounds to me like your problem isn't with the Valentine's Day card—the kid's three, so he ain't got a clue what it means, anyway—but with the two gay dads. I mean, would you be as freaked out if it were a boy with straight parents who'd sent it? Probably not. You'd probably think it was cute. So you need to sit yourself down, remind yourself the world has changed a lot in the past few fears, and get over it, to be honest with you.

II: ADVANCED PARENTING

Dear Dr. Ozzy:

I found porn on my son's computer. What should I do?
Liz, Los Angeles

I once found girlie magazines in my son's room, but what was I going to say to him? *I'm Ozzy fucking Osbourne.* Luckily, you don't have that problem—although the answer to your question really depends on your son's age. If he's 12, then I don't think he should have unlimited access to a computer with an Internet connection. But if he's 16 or older then I think it's completely normal for him to be interested in that kind of thing—as long as it ain't the really crazy freaky stuff.

The fact is, even most grown men like the occasional blue movie. I watch 'em on the road from time to time, 'cos it's better than picking up some groupie and having my balls turn green (not to mention the fact that I'm a happily married man). It can't hurt to talk to your kid about all this, though, if you can pluck up the courage. Better yet, have his father or a male friend strike up a conversation about it. Being open is usually the best way.

Dear Dr. Ozzy,
My daughter has an enormous nose. I'm not going to lie: it's **huge** *(although she has always looked beautiful to me). She says it's ruining her social life, and now she wants a nose job for her 14th birthday, which I'm told is normal these days. Advice?*
Zan, Florida

There are a lot of people who'll tell you that bullying makes you stronger and that you've gotta learn to take it if you want to get on in the world. The trouble is, though, when you're being called "big nose" five hundred times a day at school because you've got Mount Everest stuck to your face, that ain't very fucking helpful. Like everything, the people who are so sure you've got to put up with it don't have to handle the problem themselves. And kids can be incredibly cruel, y'know? Not only that, but things you get teased for a school can mess you up for the rest of your life. To this day, I'm still very insecure about my dyslexia, because I was brought up being told that I was stupid. So look: people get birth-marks and other harmless stuff removed all the time because of the way they look. It's no different with a giant conk. Buy her the nose job.

Dear Dr. Ozzy:
My 10-year-old daughter borrowed my iPad without asking and found an explicit photograph of me and my girlfriend on it (I'm

recently divorced from her mum). Now she won't speak to me—and
I'm terrified of what my ex-wife is going to do. Help!
Jerry, Milton Keynes

Adopt the brace position and prepare for bollocking of a lifetime—and to be honest with you, I ain't exactly overflowing with sympathy. I mean, I'm useless when it comes to iThis and iThat, but it doesn't take a fucking genius to realise that you need to set a password before leaving a computer lying around, especially if there are kids in the house. Mind you, taking those dirty pictures in the first place wasn't a very clever idea, either: *you're* the one who's supposed to warning your kids about "sexting," not the other way around. The divorce only makes things worse, 'cos your daughter was probably feeling weird and insecure about your new relationship to begin with. When she can finally look you in the eye again, you need to have a heart-to-heart. And while you ain't by any means in the clear yourself, you need to explain to her that some things are private, and that she can't look at your stuff without permission. Point out to her that when she gets older, she'll expect *you* to give her some personal space, too.

Dear Dr. Ozzy:
I suspect that my 15-year-old son is partaking in a bit of the old "sweet leaf"—ie, cannabis. Without alienating our good relationship, how can I deal with the, ahem, **irony** *of it all?*
"Lonnie," Channel Islands

Here's what I always tell myself: we were all kids once, and when we were worried about being caught doing anything bad, we'd lie. When my father gave me the, "If I ever catch you smoking cigarettes..." lecture, I still did it, but under wraps, so he wouldn't find out. So don't be militant about the drugs. Just come clean with your son, lay your cards on the table. Say, "Look, I know about the pot, and I'm *worried*." Tell them that unlike the dickhead who's been selling them weed, you love them unconditionally, and you're the best friend they'll ever have. It's better to be cool with your kids than put up a brick wall, otherwise they'll just go sneaking around behind your back.

Dear Dr. Ozzy:

I recently discovered that my 13-year-old daughter has been text-messaging racy photographs of herself to her boyfriend—"sexting," as it's known. What on earth should I do?

Janice, North London

Get everyone in a room together—you, your daughter, your daughter's father, the boyfriend, the boyfriend's parents—and deliver a category-five bollocking. Ram it home to them how stupid it is. Then make absolutely sure that all copies of those pictures are destroyed. The thing you need to make clear is that you aren't angry with them so much for exploring their bodies—kids have always played "doctors and nurses"—but because when you press "send" on a phone or a computer, you lose control of that image forever. All it takes is for some idiot to pick up the boyfriend's phone and forward the picture, and it could have gone around the world twice in a few hours— and ended up on the kind of websites you don't even want to believe exist. That's not even to mention the embarrassment she'd suffer if any of her classmates got hold of it.

Dear Dr. Ozzy:

My teenage son has started to spend hours alone in his bedroom, and when I go in there to clean, I notice crusty stains on the carpet. How can I tell him to use a tissue?

Anne, Edinburgh

Ask him if he's been making any Airfix planes recently, because you're finding glue all over the place. Then tell him very nicely that you don't mind him making Airfix planes—

it's normal at his age—but if he spills any *more* glue, he really should use a tissue, because it's only polite. With any luck he'll be so embarrassed, he'll never dirty the carpet again.

Dear Dr. Ozzy:
My 25-year-old daughter lives alone in London and has started to go out on Internet dates. Is this safe? How can I get her to meet a man the old-fashioned way—ie, offline?
Max, Hull

The Internet makes me glad I've got attention deficit disorder, 'cos otherwise I'd be as glued to the screen as everyone else, getting up to no good. But the truth is, times have changed, and I've heard a lot of stories about people meeting the love of their lives online—so it can't be *all* bad. Besides, what's worse, arranging dates on the computer, or getting picked up in bars? The only thing I'd say to your daughter is, "Look, a guy can tell you anything he wants to online, so *don't believe everything you read.* Plus, most guys want a bonk, not a wife." Bearing that in mind, I hope she finds the right bloke.

Dear Dr. Ozzy:
My son has taking up smoking to impress a new girlfriend. How can I get him to stop?
Lauren, Staffordshire

I made the same mistake myself. I took some chick from Digbeth to the pictures when I was 14, and brought along five cigarettes and a penny book of matches to impress her. You could smoke yourself blue in the face at the cinema in those days. So there I was, sitting in this darkened room, puffing away, trying to be Jack the lad, and suddenly I broke out in a cold sweat. *What the fuck's wrong with me?* I thought. Then I burped and tasted puke. I had to run to the can and lock myself in a stall while I coughed my guts up. I was *so* sick, man. Eventually I dragged myself out of the exit and went straight home, throwing up the whole way. To this day, I don't know what happened to the girl. I wouldn't have touched another cigarette for as long as I lived if it hadn't been the "normal" thing to do back then. So here's my suggestion: put your son off cigarettes by making him ill. Throw some ash on his cornflakes. Maybe that'll work.

Dear Dr. Ozzy:
Like you, I'm covered in tattoos, but now my beautiful 17-year-old daughter wants to get one done. I'm trying to talk her out of it, because I hate the way tattoos look on young girls, but I feel like a hypocrite. Please help.
Tony, Los Angeles

The trouble with tattoos is, they're addictive. I've known girls who start out with a little flower on their ankle, and three months later, they've got an entire battle scene across their arse. When my own daughter got tattoos, I said to her, "Look, fashions come and fashions go, and one day you might end up resenting what you did to your body when you were young." It's one think being young and beautiful with a tattoo, and another thing when you're a grandma with a floppy old dagger on your arm. I mean, there are times when even I wake up and look at the smiley face I drew on my knee and think, "What did I do *that* for?" They hurt like crazy, too, when you first get 'em done. To me, though, the best thing to point out to your daughter is that tattoos just aren't that special anymore: everyone has 'em. If she wants to be really ahead of the pack, she'd be better off investing her money in one of those laser removal companies. They're gonna be making a fortune in a few years time, when tattoos ain't the "in" thing any more.

Dear Dr. Ozzy,

My son has failed (or near enough) all his high school exams. The only career option for him now is manual labour, but he doesn't seem to care. How can I motivate him to do better?
Brian, Cheshire

I was the same when I was a kid—and it wasn't until 20 years later that I found out it was all related to my dyslexia and ADHD (attention deficit hyperactivity disorder). Your son should get checked out for both those things, 'cos there's a lot of help available now. The good news is that it's never too late to get an education these days, thanks to computers and the internet. When I was at school, 300 years ago, it was different: when you were out on yer ear, you were out on yer ear. It was the factory, or signing up as cannon fodder in the military. And they wouldn't even let me in the Army. "We want subjects, not *objects*," they told me. Fortunately, I found something I loved with heavy metal. That's the secret, really: finding something you actually enjoy doing, which can also pay the bills. At the end of the day, that matters more than passing any test.

Dear Dr. Ozzy:

My 16-year-old son says he's gay, but I think it's just the crowd he's hanging out with. Is there anything I can do—like hiring an escort, maybe—that might change his mind?
Neil, Brighton

To be honest with you, Neil, I take my hat off to your son for coming out to his old man at such a young age. That takes serious balls, and I very much doubt he'd go to all the bother if he wasn't a thousand million per cent sure. I mean, I have a gay relative, and he told me that he *always* knew he was gay, from as young as he could remember. Hiring an escort would just be an insult—not to mention illegal and more than a bit creepy. Don't do it, man. What's important is to tell your kid you love him and support him whether he's gay, straight, bi, trans, whatever. However awkward this might be for you, it'll feel like the end of the world for him if he thinks he's being rejected.

Dear Dr. Ozzy:

Like you, I have a son from another marriage. The problem is, I find it hard to connect with him, because we've lived apart for years and we're both men, so we don't like to talk about our feelings. How can I get around this without it being embarrassing?

Nigel, Durham

This is a common problem with men. I remember trying to talk to my own dad—every time I said anything to him, it was like, "What now, son?" or "I'm busy, can we talk about this later?" But times have changed. Fathers aren't these distant, scary figures any more. Still, it can be difficult with a son you don't see very often, so what I suggest—even though I don't drink any more—is to go out for a quiet pint with him. As long as you don't get blasted, it might loosen you up a bit. At the very least, just show willingness to get together, and it'll happen naturally. Whatever you do, don't put it off. Feeling embarrassed is nothing compared to the regret of missing out on your kid's life.

Dear Dr. Ozzy:

My 15-year-old daughter has started to dress in a way that would befit an employee of Spearmint Rhino in Las Vegas. How do I explain to her that this will bring her the wrong kind of male attention, without sounding like a boring old fart?

Bob, Sunderland

Unfortunately, all fathers who have girls have to go through this stage in their lives, and it ain't pleasant. Obviously you've gotta talk to her (or better yet, get her mother to talk to her).

But there's only so far you can take it, 'cos at the end of the day she might just go, "Okay, Mum and Dad, you're right," then get changed into her mini-skirt and fishnets in the garden shed, or in the back of her best mate's car. The thing is, she probably *wants* male attention—maybe there's one boy in particular she's interested in—but she has to work out for herself how to tell between the "right" and "wrong" kind. As I always say to other parents, hold on to your drawers, and hope she grows out of it.

III: SIBLINGS

Dear Dr. Ozzy:
None of my siblings get along, but they all insist on getting together every year at Christmas. I'm already dreading it—but staying away isn't an option, unless I want a war with my mother. Any tips on getting through the day?
Mike, Cornwall

If you think *your* family is bad company at Christmas, you should have been at the Osbournes' during my drinking days. It wasn't exactly merry, put it that way: by the end of the day, I'd be half-naked, covered in cranberry sauce, and throwing bricks at people. Then there was the year I bought two 28-gallon barrels of beer—bitter and mild—and set them up in my home studio. I got through both of 'em in less than a week. In fact, it got to the point where I was getting up in the night to use the toilet, and having a quick pint on my way back to bed. My ex-wife would find me the next morning, passed out in the slops. To answer your question, though: if I were you, I'd use the two rules of family gatherings—arrive early, and leave early. I understand you've got to show your face, but there's nothing to stop you keeping the torture to a minimum.

Dear Dr. Ozzy:

My dad is close to having a nervous breakdown over my 25-year-old sister's choice of boyfriend. He's is an illegal immigrant and a heavy dope smoker with (I'm not kidding) a tattoo of a pork chop and two chicken drumsticks on his chest. What can I do to put her off him?
Chaz, Birmingham

If you want someone to do something, tell them NOT to do it. This guy could be an axe-murderer, but if you say to your sister, "Look, he doesn't fit the mould" (or if you call immigration) she might just run off with him. You shouldn't lie, though, and neither should your old man: if your sister asks for approval, you should both come clean and tell her what you think. I've had all sorts come into my house over the years to see my girls... although most of the time they don't approve of *me*, not the other way around. My guess is that eventually your sister will think to herself, "What am I doing with this pork chop dickhead?" In the meantime, tell your dad to hold on, this stage will pass.

Dear Dr. Ozzy:

My brother is 30 going on 13. He has never lived on his own, and my parents won't kick him out. What can I say/do to get him to pull his head out of his backside and grow up?
Sara, Texas

When I was growing up in England, this problem was always the other way round—parents wanted their kids to look after *them*. It was the only reason why most people had kids in the first place. These days, I know grown men in their fifties who are still living their with their folks. It's fucking unbelievable, man. I mean, what happens when you want to bring a girl home to give her a good old seeing to, and your mum comes in halfway through to bring you a cup of tea and a sandwich? It doesn't exactly look very smooth does it? At the end of day, though, people do what they want to do, and there ain't much you can say to stop 'em. Especially brothers.

Although you might want to buy yours a DVD of *The 40-Year-Old Virgin*, to give him a glimpse of the future.

Dear Dr. Ozzy:
My wife's brother-in-law is a handyman/contractor, so we feel obliged to use him for all our jobs around the house. The problem is, he's useless, and he complains all the time. How can we get ourselves out of this awkward situation? (My wife sees her sister every day, so she doesn't want any tension or weirdness.)
Billy, Scarborough

If you can write to Dr. Ozzy about this, your missus can surely have a quiet word with her sister. Not, "Your husband's an incompetant, whingeing arsehole," but something more like, "Look, our two husbands have been butting heads on this DIY project, and I'm worried that if they keep at it they might fall out, and I'd really hate that to happen, so why don't we tell 'em to take a break from working together on the house for a while?" The alternative is to just put up with it—but in my experience of having renovated half the Western hemisphere with Sharon, people get very stressed-out during construction, and at some point another, voices will be raised... or worse.

IV: SPOUSES & IN-LAWS

Dear Dr. Ozzy:
I have three small kids and would love to live nearer my mum so she can help out. My husband is refusing to move, however, based on the advice of his late father to "never live in the same town as your mother-in-law." How can I change his mind?
Sonia, Paris

It's one thing saying, "I married *you*, not your mum" when you're footloose and fancy free, but it's quite another when you've got three little kids—which can feel like having three full-time jobs sometimes. If your husband's putting his foot down, then I think it's perfectly to reasonable for you to say to him, "Okay then, either you need to chip in more with the work around the house, or you need to earn more money so we can afford some extra help." Faced with a choice between his free time or his beer money, living a bit closer to your mum might suddenly begin to seem like a brilliant idea.

Dear Dr. Ozzy:
My mother-in-law is the world's worst cook. How can I avoid eating her food without offending her?
Stephanie, Durham

Get a dog. That way, you can look like a hero by filling up your plate and then coming back for more...while passing down handfuls of lumpy mashed potato to your four-legged friend under the table. Just don't get a dog that's too big: having a ten-stone Rottweiler burping and slobbering by your feet's gonna be a bit of a giveaway, especially if he farts. Another trick is to stuff the food in your pocket. One time I managed to fit all three courses of one of Sharon's dinners into my coat. The only problem was, I forgot all about it, so when she took a trip to the dry-cleaners a few months later, she found my stash of rock-hard dumplings. Most of 'em ended up being thrown at my head.

Dear Dr. Ozzy:
My wife has suddenly started going to a local "happy clappy" church. I'm not religious at all, and to be honest with you, I find it all very disturbing. Is it possible to have a marriage where one person is an atheist and the other is a devout Christian?
Oliver, Darlington

Some people turn to God like others turn to cocaine— usually 'cos there's something missing in their lives. I had a very good friend who was an addict for years, and the second he gave it up, he became a Jesus-freak. It was like he swapped one for the other. Talk to your wife about it. See if you can find out what it is that's making her so intense all of a sudden. But if she continues this way, there's gonna be a blow up at some point, mark my words. Evangelists are supposed to evangelise, so eventually she's gonna be on your case about the "good news." And that'll be very bad news for you. (After this question was published, I got an e-mail from a guy called Paul from Oxford, who said his Catholic mum and atheist dad had been together for 30 years. "The bottom line is if they have love and respect for each other," he told me. "If not, then that's where the problems start, irrespective of religious persuasion.")

Dear Dr. Ozzy:
My partner is divorced and has three kids who don't live with us. The trouble is, he **never** *stops talking about them. He even talks to me about his bloody ex-wife! It's driving me mad, but I'm afraid to mention it, in case he thinks I'm narrow-minded.*
Julia, London

I've had first-hand experience of this problem, and it's a tough one. At one point I was spending so much time juggling between my first wife, Thelma, and my second wife, Sharon, I'd come home and call the missus "Tharon"—which earned me more than a few black eyes, believe me. Over in California, you hear of these weird families where everyone's divorced and remarried but still friends, but that's gotta be pretty fucked up. I mean, we're all human. It sounds to me like you've started to feel a bit like the booby prize when it comes to your bloke. My advice would be to talk to him about it, but do in a way that doesn't sound like a criticism. Put yourself in his shoes; ask yourself what it would be like if *you* had a little boy or girl from another marriage, and how much you'd love them and want to stay in touch. But then explain to him that you have feelings, too, and that you need to know how you fit into his world.

Dear Dr. Ozzy:

My mother-in-law complains to me—in detail—about how my father-in-law fails to satisfy her in bed. What sort of brain eraser do you recommend? (I'm tempted by the Smith & Wesson method.)
Nina, Texas

As far as my kids are concerned, having sex over the age of 45 should be illegal. Never in a *million years* would I talk to them directly—never mind their partners—about giving one to their mum (although if they read this book they ain't gonna have much choice). I mean, what's wrong with this woman? No-one in their right mind wants to think about their father-in-law's one-eyed wonder, or how good he is at swinging it between the sheets. I recommend changing the conversation, or buying ear-plugs.

Dear Dr. Ozzy:

My parents don't get along with each other any more, but they're so old now—late 60s and early 70s—they don't want to divorce and end up living alone. The trouble is, their unhappiness with each other is making everyone around them miserable. Any words of wisdom?
Catherine, Boston

It's not what they should do, it's what YOU should do. Call a family meeting. I do this all the time when something's bothering me. Tell your folks that their bickering is getting everyone down, and that it's reaching the point where it's giving you so much anxiety, you don't even want to spend time with them any more—which makes you sad, 'cos you love them both very much. If they still can't resolve their problems after that, ask if they can at least make an effort to be civil to each other while you're around.

Dear Dr. Ozzy:

My wife gets very aggressive during her "time of the month," but if I point this out, she gets even angrier. What can I do about this?

Gary, London

If there are four words that a married man should never say to his wife—especially during an argument—it's "time of the month." It's the atomic bomb option, and the bomb's only ever gonna land in one place: on your fucking head. Personally, I have a lot of sympathy for women when it comes to the T.O.T.M.—it must be awful. My advice to you, Gary, is to simply get out of the house if you suspect that's what's putting your missus in a bad mood. As anyone in the Army will tell you: it's harder to hit a moving target.

Dear Dr. Ozzy,

I want to propose to my girlfriend. The trouble is, her father died ten years ago, and now she has a stepfather who she doesn't really like. Do I need to ask his permission?

Ted, Stevenage

No. But if you want to keep the peace, why not ask the mother and the stepfather at the same time? It's never a bad idea to suck up to the in-laws, 'cos if you're anything like me, at some point you're gonna need all the goodwill you can get.

Dear Dr. Ozzy:

I'm convinced my husband has fallen in love with one of his colleagues, but I don't think he's having an affair—yet. Should I do nothing, or confront him? I'd prefer it if he had a one-night stand than a close emotional relationship with another woman.

Joan, Bristol

Unless you have convincing evidence that something dodgy's going on, I'd leave it alone. Otherwise, your husband could end up saying to himself, "Oh, well she thinks I'm messing around anyway, so why not go for it?" Or you could make him defensive, and then he might start to lie, and then you'll have this big wedge between you. The absolute last thing you want to do is make it You vs. Them, 'cos that'll just make 'em closer. One sneaky tactic you could use is to befriend this woman and start hanging out with her all the time—the old "keep your enemies closer" game. Not that Sharon would ever do that, mind you. If she ever suspected anything, she'd be round the other woman's house in a heartbeat, breathing fire all over the place, and scaring the living shit out of her.

Dear Dr. Ozzy:
This will make me sound like a chauvinistic pig, but I hate the fact my wife earns far more than me. It's not like she brags, but it's driving me insane that she pays for everything, from the nanny to our family car. How can I consider myself a "real" man?
Jasper, Surrey

I know exactly how you feel. When I first started seeing Sharon, I was the smelly guy who'd pissed away all his money and been fired by his band, and she was one with diamonds and fur whose dad was a multimillionaire. It made me feel terrible. In fact, I think it would make *any* man feel terrible unless he's some kind of gigolo who preys on loaded women. It might be an old-fashioned way of looking at the world, but I don't think there's anything wrong with wanting to provide. If that ain't an option, though, you just need to make sure the missus knows you're grateful—maybe by cooking dinner, doing the dishes, giving her foot massages, etc. Whatever you do, *don't* do what I did, and steal a bunch of flowers from the nearest graveyard to give to her. It might have seemed like a good idea at the time, but it soon backfired when she realised there was a card attached—which I'd forgotten to take off. She thought it was gonna to be a romantic poem or something. Instead it said, *"In loving memory of our dearest Harry."*

Dear Dr. Ozzy:

My wife insists on going to therapy every week, but as the earner in the family, I get lumped with the bills. Now the therapist is telling my wife she needs an expensive holiday—and that she should stand up to me more on "financial issues"! So I'm paying someone to make me poorer and ruin my marriage. What should I do?

Steven, Norwich

I've been in a similar situation myself, and there's an easy solution: suggest to the missus that you go along to one of her "sessions," so you can say to the therapist in person, "Look, I resent the fact I'm forking out good cash to help my wife, and all you're doing is poisoning her against me." Or you could just punch the guy in the face, and go, "Analyse that." Seriously, though: you've gotta give your side of the story. Therapists aren't superhuman, they're just paid to listen (and make suggestions, in some cases). If your wife refuses to let you go, then it might be time to get suspicious. She could be using her weekly "sessions" as a cover up for something else, possibly involving the pool boy.

Dr. Ozzy's Trivia Quiz: Flesh & Blood

Find the answers—and your score—on page 263

1. Which well-known historic person was sold to human traffickers by his family when he was a kid?
   a) Martin Luther King
   b) Joseph from the Bible
   c) Oliver Cromwell

2. What's the most number of babies (allegedly) ever born to one woman?
   a) 71
   b) 102
   c) 69

3. In 2010, a woman in New Mexico, USA, did *what* to her daughter-in-law during a fight?
   a) Ripped off her nipple
   b) Pushed her out of a tenth-floor window
   c) Tattooed "FOR SALE" on her forehead

4. According to therapists, what is the secret to a successful marriage?
   a) Using flattery and persuasion
   b) A bonk every other day
   c) Being a total loser

5. How old was the youngest (confirmed) mother in medical history?
   a) 7
   b) 6
   c) 5

Surgery: Not Just for Professionals

5

If You Want Something Done...
Do It Yourself

Okay, before we start this chapter, I don't want anyone getting the wrong idea: I ain't saying you should go out and buy a hacksaw, a pair of barbeque tongs, and tube of Super Glue, then try and remove one of your own kidneys. If something's bothering you, and you've got any choice in the matter, *go to a fucking doctor*—a real one, not Dr. Ozzy—instead of trying to fix the problem yourself. Especially if it involves chopping something off, taking something out, or making your tits bigger.

Sometimes, though, doing it yourself is the only way to go. Like that guy who went hiking in Utah, got stuck under a rock, then had to chop off his own arm. If he hadn't been willing to get his hands dirty, he'd still be under that rock today. Then there was the famous case of that chick in Mexico who went into labour when she was all alone and in the middle of nowhere (she lived halfway up a mountain, and her husband was down the pub). She didn't want to risk going into labour, 'cos her last baby had been born dead, so she chugged half a bottle of rubbing alcohol, got out the kitchen knife, gave herself a C-Section, then passed out. The kid was fine...although he had a bit of a hangover.*

Obviously it's unlikely you'll ever find yourself in such a heavy duty situation. On the off-chance, though, I recommend tearing out the next few pages and keeping 'em with you at all times.

———

Dear Dr. Ozzy:

I think my arm is broken, but I don't have health insurance (I live in the United States) and I don't want to end up getting a bill for thousands of dollars from a hospital emergency room. Is there a fail-safe (and painless) way to make your own plaster-cast?

Stephen, Florida

Okay Stephen, this is what you have to do: get yourself down to the local Wal-Mart and buy three paper cups, some sticky-backed plastic, a pen, four knitting needles, and a ball of string. You'll also need a lemon, some ice, and tube of toothpaste. Oh, and a bag of cement mix. Lay it all out on the kitchen table. Then take a deep breath. When you've done all that...GO. TO. A. DOCTOR. Honestly, are you fucking *mad*? Even if you don't have any dough, the E.R. will still treat you, and you can deal with the debt-collectors later. Trust me, your arm is going to be a lot more useful than any cash you might lose.

———

*I ain't making this up. The mum's name is Ines Ramirex Perez, and she had the baby on March 5, 2000 (according to the Associated Press).

Dear Dr. Ozzy:

If I ever had to remove my own leg in an emergency (say, I was trapped under something heavy while a long way from home, as in the movie 127 Hours), how difficult would it be?

Jay, Los Angeles

Depends. If you had a chainsaw handy, it wouldn't be difficult at all—apart from the screaming agony part. Also, it goes without saying that you'd have to be pretty fucking sure there were no other options before you went all-in. The last thing you'd want is go to all the bother of amputating your own leg, only for ten fire engines to pull up three minutes later. In terms of the technicalities, I can only tell you what I saw on *127 Hours*: you need to make a tourniquet; saw through the skin, flesh and muscle; find a way to break the bone (or bones); then snip the tendons. Then you've gotta find help before dying of blood loss or infection. In other words, it's best avoided, if at all possible.

DR. OZZY'S INSANE-BUT-TRUE STORIES

DIY Surgery—What NOT to Try...

◆ Self-circumcision with a pair of old nail clippers. A bloke in Hertfordshire tried this in 2009 and ended up in the emergency ward with a plaster cast on his knob. "This is something we would advise men *never* to attempt," said the hospital. No fucking shit, man.

◆ Gastric bypass operation using a kit you bought on Amazon.com. This ain't a joke: a company in America was actually selling "Laparoscopic Gastric Bypass Kits" on the internet until recently. It was all a big mistake, apparently: the kit was only supposed to be available to hospitals. Still, it got 38 "user reviews"—all of 'em from people taking the piss.

◆ Brain surgery. A bit of an obvious one this, I would have thought—but not to a chick in Gloucester who drilled a hole in her own head while standing in front of a mirror (with a video camera running), 'cos she'd been told it might cure "tiredness." It all went well apart from the fact she put a big fucking hole in her head (although there can't have been much grey matter there to begin with). Afterwards, she insisted she felt much better.

◆ Laser eyesight correction. The main problem with zapping your own eyeballs is that you need your eyeballs to make sure you're pointing the laser at the right part of your eyeballs... it's also pretty hard to get your hands on a reliable laser, unless you live in a volcano and answer to the name "Blofeld." The one in your old CD player ain't gonna do much good.

Dear Dr. Ozzy:
I want to look like a celebrity but can't afford the high cost of getting my acne scars removed by a surgeon. If I buy my own silicone on the Internet, could I simply treat the scars myself (I've seen how doctors on reality TV shows do the injections)?
Jaynie, London

No, no, fuck no, absolutely no way, and NO again. Times a million. I saw Neil Armstrong land on the moon on the telly, but that doesn't mean I could pilot the Mars Rover, does it? I've heard terrible stories about people buying the wrong kind of silicone—like the stuff they put in car engines—and shooting themselves up with it, only to end up looking like Freddy Krueger from *Nightmare on Elm Street*. The worst thing is, you can't just leave it in there: someone has to cut open your face and get it out. To be honest with you, though, I'm not even sure your acne scars are the real problem. If you're obsessed enough about your looks that you're willing to stick a needle in yourself, there might be something else going on. In fact, I would recommend talking to a therapist, 'cos it might be that you're suffering from some kind of negative body image disorder. I ain't got anything against plastic surgery—I've had it done myself, and so has my wife—but sometimes people get way too hung up on this stuff.

Dr. Ozzy:
I crushed my finger between two heavy steel pipes: now it's swollen and black. Do you think it's broken?
Phil, Essex

This question isn't as stupid as it sounds, 'cos I once broke my tibia—my shinbone—and I didn't realise it for weeks. I thought I was just bruised or something. Mind you, I was so blasted all the time, you could have taken a chainsaw to my right arm and I probably wouldn't have noticed. In fact, I think the reason I broke my tibia in the first place is because I was off my nut and fell down a flight of stairs. The other problem was, no-one ever used to listen to me when I complained about breaking something, because they all knew I saw it as an excuse to get my hands on some pain pills, which meant I could get even more out of my skull. I was like the boy who cried wolf, y'know? Especially when we were in America. I mean, you can't go a doctor in the states for *anything* without coming away with a bottle of pills. I used to turn up at appointments with a fucking shopping trolley. And in my darkest days, I used to actually *try* to injure myself to get pills. Which brings me back to the question: if you're asking me if your finger's broken, you're obviously not the kind of person who tries to scam your doctors, so if I were you, I'd go and get it X-rayed. Either that, or go out and play a couple of games of pool. You'll know if it's broken or not after that.

Dear Dr. Ozzy:

I have a corn on my right foot, and after a lot of consideration, I'm thinking of trimming it myself. Are there any risks I should know about?
Gian, Frosinone, Italy

Don't do it, man. Seriously. I had a hairdresser once who got some kind of growth on his foot, so he dealt with it himself, forgot about it for years, then found out—too late—that it was cancer. The other thing you've gotta bear in mind is, your entire body is weighing down on that foot for most of the day, so if things go wrong in that area, it can have consequences you can't even imagine. I mean, if you got a blow-out on your car, would you get out your little bicycle repair kit, glue the hole back together, then head out on the motoroway? No. So get yourself to a doctor—or better yet, a chiropodist.

Dear Dr. Ozzy:

Is it really true that a Russian GP stationed in Antarctica removed his own appendix, spent only a fortnight recovering, then carried on with his work? Could anyone basically perform a self-appendectomy if there were no other help available?
Gillian, Spain

I got someone to look this up for me, and as mind-blowing as it sounds, it's absolutely true. It ain't the only case, either. Another doctor in America took out his own appendix just to prove that his anaesthetic worked (it's a good job the guy wasn't selling guns for a living—he might have ended up shooting himself in the head to prove his bullets worked). Just because a few nutters have managed to slice themselves open doesn't mean anyone else should try it, though—no matter what the circumstances. Unless you've got a set of mirrors handy, some sharp knives, a bag of hardcore antibiotics, and a pair of balls the size of Mount Rushmore, you'd be better off using your energy to find medical attention before you start digging around in your own stomach with a Swiss Army Knife. I mean, could you honestly say you'd even know what an appendix looked like? Knowing me, I'd end up cutting out a lung instead.

Dr. Ozzy's Trivia Quiz: Under the Knife

Find the answers—and tote up your score—on page 263

1. Which of these horrendous medical errors really happened?
   a) Amputating the wrong leg
   b) Bifurcation (which left the patient with a forked tongue)
   c) Transplanting the wrong heart and lungs

2. Which of these DIY cosmetic surgeries did people *really* attempt?
   a) A nose job with a chisel and a chicken bone
   b) Double chin surgery with a bread knife and a vacuum cleaner
   c) Lip augmentation with an injection of "sexual lubricant"

3. What does "auto-enucleation" mean?
   a) Deliberately exposing yourself to radiation
   b) Gouging out your own eyes
   c) When you body rejects an anaesthetic

4. In Medieval times, who did you go to for surgery?
   a) A barber
   b) A blacksmith
   c) A carpenter

5. Which of these famous medical cases resulted in death...
   a) The man who removed his own pacemaker
   b) The man who deliberately cycled into the back of a truck to fracture his jaw, so it could be reset in a "more attractive" way
   c) The woman who tried to give herself liposuction by cutting her thighs and squeezing out the fat

General Practise

6

Dr. Ozzy's A-to-Z of
Uncommon Complaints

Every day, people write to me about the craziest shit you've ever heard in your life. A lot of the questions are so far-out, it's impossible to sort them into any normal categories. That's why I've put all the whacky stuff into this chapter and listed them alphabetically—so if you swallow a tennis ball, get a screwdriver stuck in your right ear, or start vomiting through your eyeballs, all you've gotta do is look under the right letter, and hope you find the answer. Personally, I wish I'd had a guide like this for myself over the years, 'cos it would have come in very handy that time when my right leg started to dance a jig all by itself (look under "J" for "Jimmy Legs"), or when I accidentally ate a bumblebee on the way to the pub (see "F" for "Flies & Other Insects'"). Oh, you'll also find some "Surgery Noticeboard" announcements in between the Q&As: we print these in *The Sunday Times Magazine* whenever we get a ton of e-mails on one subject. As a fake newspaper doctor with fuck-all qualifications, I'm always happy to pass along other people's dodgy advice.

———————————

A.

Animals (Effect on Mood)

Dear Dr. Ozzy:
My dog, Clive (a Labrador), seems awfully glum, to the point where it's beginning to get me down. Could he be suffering from doggie depression? If so, what can I do about it?
Amy, Lille, France

Doggie Prozac—ask your vet about it. Personally, the only doggie depression I've ever experienced is the feeling I get after one of my four-legged friends takes a dump behind the sofa.

Animals (Effect on Sleep)

Dear Dr. Ozzy:
Every night I go to bed with my dog, Ozzy (named after you), but wake up at 4am. I really want to stay in bed longer, but no matter what I do, I can't get back to sleep. Is this something to do with Ozzy, do you think? Please help, it's driving me crazy.
Sammy [No address given]

I don't see how one dog could be much of an issue—I go to bed with 17 dogs, plus about 20 mobile phones, and the wife. It sounds to me more like you've got a sleep disorder. I've had the same problem for years, so I got someone to come over to the house one evening, put all these electrode things on my head, hook them up to a computer, and see what was going on in my brain. He was up all night, this guy, twiddling his knobs and studying his graphs—he must be a raging insomniac himself—and when the results came back, my doc put me on a mild anti-depressant which helps me nod-off easier. It beats sleeping pills. Or whacking myself on the head with a mallet.

B.

Brain (Use Of)

Dear Dr. Ozzy:
Is it true that humans use only 10 per cent of their brains, or is this just another one of those stupid myths?
Andrew, Kent

I fucking hope that ain't the case, 'cos I've only got about ten per cent of my brain *left*. By your definition, that means I'm running on about one per cent these days. Actually...that explains a lot.

Breath (Offensive)

Dear Dr. Ozzy:
My breath is really bad—to the point where I can't talk to people who are close to me. I'm a student here in Ghana, and I find it difficult even just to say "Hello" to friends on campus, because I just don't want to embarrass myself. Please Dr. Ozzy, I need your help. . . .
Emmanuel, Ghana

A long time ago, I made a pact with my wife: if my breath is bad, she has to tell me—and vice versa. Obviously no-one needs to break the news to *you*, Emmanuel. By the sound of it, when you open your mouth, the sun gags. My guess is that the problem is being caused by one of two things: something very nasty in your gut, or gum disease. If I were you, my first stop would be a dentist—although you might want to give her some advance warning, so she can put on a rubber suit and face mask, and light a few candles around the room first. In the meantime, try Euthymol, an old English brand of toothpaste, which makes you feel like you just gargled with gasoline and lit a match. Also buy some ultra-strength mouthwash, like Listerine, and get yourself a tongue scraper.

Burping (Potential Side Effects Of)

Dear Dr. Ozzy:
A friend told me that burping too hard can rip a hole in your stomach, is this true?
Anna (12 years old), Long Island, New York
   No. I wouldn't have any stomach left if that were the case. In fact, I once saw a bloke on telly who could talk and burp at the same time. I tried to do it myself once, but ended up puking into Sharon's handbag. Lesson: some things are best left to the professionals.

Bedbugs

Dear Dr. Ozzy:
My husband and I have developed such a paralyzing fear of bedbugs that we've become like prisoners in our own home. How can we get over our paranoia?
Tara, West Village, New York
   I've never had a problem with bedbugs—probably 'cos they take one sip of my blood and drop dead from all the toxic shit in there. But I understand your concern: no-one wants to wake up with a thousand little red bite marks on their ballsack. Just bear in mind that bedbugs aren't the worst thing in the world. I'm about to go to South America, for example, and I'm told they have these "kissing spiders": they crawl up your body and onto your face, squat over your lips, secrete an anaesthetic, suck out the blood, take a dump, then scamper away back to their holes. Meanwhile, the spider crap contains a kind of bacteria that literally eats your heart out. I'm so freaked out about it, I'm probably gonna spend the whole tour sleeping in a sealed Ziploc fucking bag.

C.

Cancer (Coping With)

Dear Dr. Ozzy:

In the past five years, I've had two hip operations, throat cancer, and now a serious heart problem. As a result of chemo and radiotherapy I can eat only liquid food through a syringe into my stomach, and sex is impossible because of the beta blockers I take for my ticker. Thankfully I can still drink beer, but otherwise I'm rapidly losing my sense of humour, which isn't like me. How can I cheer myself up?
Charlie (65 years old), Devon

This is one of the reasons why medical marijuana ain't necessarily such a bad idea. I mean, anyone who reads "Ask Dr. Ozzy" on a regular basis knows that I always tell people to steer clear of weed 'cos you never know how strong it is, or how you'll react (never mind that it's illegal)—but over in Los Angeles, a lot of people with heavy-duty medical problems say that prescription pot helps them with everything from muscle pain to getting their appetites back. My advice is to talk to your doctor, keep drinking the beer, and try to find something else, *anything*, that gives you a break from the discomfort. It sounds like you've had some rotten luck, Charlie, and I wish you all the best.

Chewing Gum (Ingested)

Dear Dr. Ozzy:

I just swallowed a piece of chewing gum. Is it true this will take seven years to pass through my system?
Frank, Portsmouth

That can't be true, otherwise I'd be half-human, half-spearmint by now.

Cruise Ships (Downsides Of)

Dear Dr. Ozzy:
My wife wants to go on an expensive cruise ship holiday—but I'm afraid of getting food poisoning, falling overboard, or being seasick. Am I being too paranoid?
Tyler, Atlanta

No, you ain't. I took the *QE2* to America once with Sharon, 'cos she was pregnant and couldn't fly. I was so out of my fucking mind with boredom, it would have been a *relief* to fall overboard, quite frankly. In the end I begged the ship's doc to give me something to knock me out. When I finally woke up in New York, Sharon was so angry, she tried to throw me through one of the portholes. I've never been on a cruise ship again.

Crying (During Urination)

Dear Dr. Ozzy:
I cry when I urinate. Tears literally stream from my eyes, like I'm peeling an onion. It is not painful nor anything, but I'm worried I have a rare disease. What's your expert advice?
Pierre, Barcelona

No offence, Pierre, but this is really fucking weird. Here's my prescription: 1) Keep a box of tissues in the can, and 2) Get a second opinion, ideally from someone whose name ain't Ozzy Osbourne.

D.

Death (Stress Related To)

Dear Dr. Ozzy:
My fiancé of two years—a wealthy Arab man—has been told he has terminal cancer. After trying to ignore the subject, I asked about his will (I'm no longer working because of the economic crisis). He

told me that because he hates his family, he's giving everything to charity. When I asked about me, he said I would get nothing either. I told him I was hurt, but he said he was more hurt, because he's dying, and I asked him for money (I did feel like a jerk for asking, but I need a place to live). Who's in the right?
Margaret, London

It sounds to me like your fiancé is angry about dying—it's hard to blame him—and he's lashing out. But you shouldn't feel like a jerk, either. I mean, if the bloke's giving all his money away to his cocker spaniel (or whatever his favourite charity is), who's going to pay for his funeral? Is he happy to think he'll be tossed into some government-run pit with a cardboard headstone? And if he cared about you enough to get engaged, why does he want you out on the street? Fair enough, he doesn't have to give you every last penny he earned during his lifetime, but sorting out your digs for a year or two, to make sure you can get back on your feet, ain't too much to ask. I can't stress enough that people need to get these things down in writing early on, before a situation like this comes up. It's normal to want to put anything related to death on the back-burner, but *everyone* needs a will. It ain't very nice talking about the Final Curtain, but it's a lot worse to have the conversation when you're coping with a tragedy.

Dentistry (Basic Techniques)

Dear Dr. Ozzy,
I've been getting a lot of severe headaches recently and have been told that they could be caused by teeth-grinding. Is it possible to grind your teeth without knowing it?
Jennifer, Northumberland

You and I have exactly the same problem. I started getting these really bad headaches a few weeks ago, and being a hypochondriac, I thought, "Right, that's it, I've got a brain tumour." I was one stage away from buying myself a casket when my GP told me that I needed to see a dentist, not an oncologist. So that's what I did, and now I've got these little rubber things to put over my teeth at night, so I don't grind them in my sleep—which, to answer your question, is supposedly very common. I don't wear them half the time, though, 'cos it's a major ball-ache putting them in. I'd rather take an aspirin.

Dear Dr. Ozzy:

If I rinse my mouth out with descaling solution (like the stuff you use to clean out a coffee machine), will it get rid of my plaque? I ask because my dental hygienist charges a fortune to do the same thing, and I'm trying to economize.

Peter, Lowestoft, Suffolk

If you think a scrape and polish is a rip-off, just wait and see how much they charge the idiot who comes in with no teeth left 'cos he gargled with sodium tripolyphosphate. They'll still be sending you bills when you're six feet under. In fact, this reminds me of the time one of my good friends tried to cure a rash on his Honourable Gentleman with bleach, 'cos he didn't want to have to admit to his family GP that he'd been unfaithful to his wife. Needless to say, his missus soon found out what was going on, 'cos he spent the next month in hospital, screaming in pain.

Dear Dr. Ozzy:

You and your lovely wife have great teeth... so white! What I'd like to know is: would you recommend using shop-bought whitening agents? As a smoker who drinks too much coffee, I'm badly in need of a non-celebrity solution.

Freda, Milton Keynes

I hate to break it to you, Freda, but my choppers ain't real. All my teeth are screwed in: for cleaning, they just unscrew 'em and give 'em a good polishing. They ain't falsies—they're implants. I started out with caps, which means they file down your teeth to posts and cement fake crowns on top of them. But then the posts rotted away, so they gave me implants, which are attached to my jaws with titanium screws. If I had my real teeth, I'd look like Herman Munster's ugly brother. I think growing up in Britain is partly to blame—I mean, we're not exactly renowned for our teeth, are we? Even Harley Street dentists aren't that good. I went to a bloke who does the royals' teeth once, and I came out of the place looking like a racehorse. But the biggest problem for me was being a drug addict: it kills all your calcium, which is what keeps your mouth healthy. Getting back to your question, though: I ain't got a clue about whitening agents, but it can't do any harm to give them a go, can it? As for a "non-celebrity solution," the good news is that you don't have to be *famous* to see a dentist in Beverly Hills...

You just need a ton of dough.

Doctors (Issues Regarding)

Dear Dr. Ozzy:

Do you think people should be allowed to rate their doctors on the internet, like they can rate albums—or do you think the medical profession is too important to be subjected to the kind of abuse you got in 1970 for the first Black Sabbath LP?

Sally, Glasgow

Honestly? I don't know. I mean, my GP might give me a drug for something, and I might get better with no side-effects. Another person might get exactly the same treatment, and his head might swell up to ten times its normal size. So would it be fair if the guy with the massive head gave the doc a bad review? Probably not. Then again, if you were gonna have heart surgery, and the reviews told you that your surgeon's last ten patients had croaked it on the operating table, you'd want to know that. The way I see it, though, a doctor spends years

and years and serious amounts of dough to become qualified
to make life or death decisions—so it ain't fair if one person
with a bee up their arse can ruin his career with a review that
takes three seconds to write.

Dear Dr. Ozzy:
*Like you, I've always been a bit of a hypochondriac. However, for the
past 20-odd years (since my parents died, and my newborn son needed
heart surgery) I've had a phobia of anything to do with doctors, and
I avoid them as long as the pain doesn't become unbearable. My
head tells me that I should take your advice and benefit from modern
medicine, but unfortunately the coward in me is stronger. Any advice?*
Christine, Germany

If you're too afraid to go to the doctor 'cos it brings back
painful memories—or 'cos you're worried that you'll get bad
news—there's only one solution: *don't go.* Simple as that. Go
to the pub instead. At the end of the day, Christine, only you
can make the decision. The thing is, though, if you're afraid
of getting bad news, isn't it better to get it earlier rather than
later? The only reason my wife is still alive is because she got
bad news early. That meant she was able to get to her cancer
before it spread any further and killed her. And, speaking for
myself, if I don't go to the doctor on a regular basis, I'll just
drive myself nuts about every little twinge and ache. It sounds
to me like you're already worrying yourself sick. So why not
take a deep breath and make an appointment?

Dribble (Excessive)

Dear Dr. Ozzy:
*I've started to drool at night while asleep, meaning I wake up every
morning to an unpleasantly damp pillow. Is this normal at my age
(early 60s, like you), and is there a cure?*
John, Essex

Believe me, there are much worse ways to wake up in the morning than with a soggy pillow. If you've reached your early sixties and that's the only thing you've got to complain about, I think you're doing pretty well, to be honest with you. As for a cure—try blow-drying the inside of mouth dry before going to bed. Or put a raincoat over your pillowcase.

E.

Ears (Ringing In)

Dear Dr. Ozzy:
I have two boys in a metal band and they've been practicing in my home for the past four years. Now I have ringing in my ears. Any advice?
Grace, Miami

A classic case of heavy *metal-itus*. I suffer from permanent tinnitus because of all the headbanging I've done over the years—which means I've now got this constant ringing in my ears, like a "WEEEE!!" noise, but louder. It's also made me somewhat deaf (or "conveniently deaf," as Sharon calls it). The sad thing is that there's an easy way to prevent tinnitus, and it's called buying a pair of earplugs. Do it now, before the damage gets worse.

Eyelids (Quivering)

Dear Dr. Ozzy:
When I'm very tired, my eyelids quiver. It's quite embarrassing—is there a way of stopping it?
Lucy, New York

You've gotta listen to your body, man. If you stayed up all night and ended up with a headache and an upset stomach, you wouldn't think twice about what to do: *you'd go to bed*. But a lot of people who only get five or six hours of shut-eye every night can't believe it when they need half a gallon of espresso just to get out of bed the next morning. Clearly, in your case, your body is screaming at you that it wants more rest. I'm exactly the same way: I might be the Prince of Darkness, but if I don't get my afternoon nap, I'm useless for the rest of the day. That's why Europeans invented the siesta.

F.

Farts (Storage Of)

Dear Dr. Ozzy:
A new book claims that during the Great Plague of London in 1665, people were told to store their farts in a jar and sniff them if they felt unwell. Have you ever attempted to do this? How would one go about storing an outbreak of gas in an enclosed space?
Ellen, Beijing

It always blows my mind, the things people used to do to themselves before modern medicine. Could you imagine, sitting on the sofa with a cup of tea and the newspaper, going, "Darling, pass the jam jar, I've got a bit of a headache." Then again, if you didn't have aspirin, what were you supposed to do? And no, I've never tried this myself—I might be crazy, but I ain't *that* crazy. When an ill wind blows in my house, I'm more worried about opening the windows before Sharon gets home than trying to save it for later.

Flies & Other Insects (Swallowed)

Dear Dr. Ozzy:
I recently swallowed a fly while horse riding. Now I'm in a panic: will give me an awful disease?
Nicola, East Finchley, London

I know how you feel: I was riding a motorcycle once with the visor up, and a bumblebee went down my throat. Not that it felt like a bumblebee, mind you—at the speed I was going, I thought I'd swallowed a fucking pigeon. People think that eating a bat is bad, but, believe me, inhaling a bee at 70mph is worse. The next day my epiglottis swelled up to three times it's normal size and I had to get an injection. Now, that wouldn't happen with a fly. But the big problem with a fly is, you know it hasn't being doing anything pleasant lately: it certainly ain't been down the local spa, drinking honeysuckle tea. Flies eat turdburgers and bathe in their own throw-up. But don't freak out too much. Remember, cats eat flies all the time, and it never seems to do *them* any harm. So give it a few days, and if you feel okay, you've probably got the all-clear.

G.

Germs (Public Loos)

Dear Dr. Ozzy:
What's the point in washing your hands in a public loo if you have to open the door on the way out using a handle that's been touched by hundreds or thousands of other people who didn't wash their hands? I've tried getting around the problem by pulling my sleeve over my hand when I touch the door, but that's disgusting, too.
Chris, Newcastle

At last—I've found someone else who gets as freaked out about this as I do. I can't fucking stand it: there you are, scrubbing your hands at the sink, but then to get out of the bog you have to grab a handle that the guy in front of you who didn't bother to scrub up has already used. I mean, let's face it, the average door knob in a public toilet has seen more dick than a Turkish knocking shop. Like you, I've also tried using my sleeve—but all you're doing is putting the germs somewhere else. I get so wound-up about it, I've been known to rip the entire roll of paper towel off the wall and use that. But the point is, *you shouldn't have to*—they should make the doors in public toilets swing OUT, so you can open them with your foot. It ain't fucking rocket science. That way, you go in there, wash your hands, do your business, wash your hands again, then you're on your way, germ-free. If I were Prime Minister, this would be my first law.

Dear Dr. Ozzy,
Regarding unhygienic door handles: I've come up with a design (patent pending) for a new kind of germ-free knob—when squeezed, it releases a dab of antiseptic liquid into your palm. Might this solve the problem? *
Tranquility, Oxford
    As long as I didn't end up with a hand like a snail's arse for the rest of the day, then yes. (Maybe the antiseptic stuff could be a spirit, so it evaporates?)

DR. OZZY'S SURGERY NOTICEBOARD

The Trouble with Dirty Knobs

◆ Judging by the number of e-mails I keep getting about germ-covered door handles, I obviously ain't the only one who has a serious bee up my arse on this issue. James in Aberdeen says the solution is "mind-numbingly obvious: automatic doors. They should be

---

*See diagram on page 110.

law." (I 1,000 per cent agree). Meanwhile, Mike in Glasgow says doors aren't even necessary: "You just need an L-shaped entrance, so passing perverts can't peek." Pete in Merseyside has more practical advice—"Always use your pinkie to open lav doors: you're unlikely to ever put your smallest finger in your mouth." (Unless your name happens to be Dr. Evil, Pete). Alternatively, Marion from Aberystwyth says the trick is to "grab a few sheets of toilet roll to protect your hands when opening the door, then dispose of them when you're done." She also suggests: "Disposable gloves should be provided in vending machines as you enter the bathroom." Special thanks go to Gill in Cornwall, who did a Miss Marple and counted every single bloke who entered and exited the public bog at Cartgate picnic area in Somerset, England, over the course of the weekend, then e-mailed me the results (it was a long e-mail). "Judging by the length of time they took inside, none of them washed and dried their hands—because using the apparatus to do that takes about five minutes!" she concluded. This is the reason why people like me, who actually use the sink, get so pissed off: *what's the point of washing and drying if you've then got to touch something that's got the germs of a thousand dicks on it?* Finally, John from Bristol got in touch to argue (as I've also done) that building regulations need to be re-written, making it law that public toilet doors are hung the other way around. That way, our feet can do all the dirty work. David Cameron, are you listening...

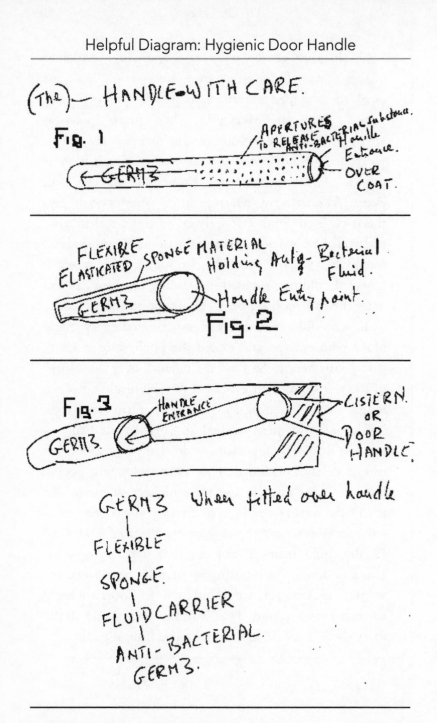

(The) — HANDLE-WITH CARE.

Fig. 1

APERTURES TO RELEASE ANTI-BACTERIAL substance.

Handle Entrance.

OVER COAT.

← GERMS

FLEXIBLE ELASTICATED SPONGE MATERIAL Holding Anta-Bacterial Fluid.

GERMS

Handle Entry point.

Fig. 2

Fig. 3

HANDLE ENTRANCE

GERMS.

CISTERN. OR DOOR HANDLE.

GERMS When fitted over handle
|
FLEXIBLE
|
SPONGE.
|
FLUID CARRIER
|
ANTI-BACTERIAL.
GERMS.

Dear Dr. Ozzy:
What do you make of this craze for using hand-sanitizers obsessively throughout the day? I mention it because I had to shake someone's hand at the beginning of a business meeting recently and they hadn't got rid of all the lotion, so I was left with a sticky palm. I found the whole thing quite offensive, to be honest with you.
Eamon, Limerick, Ireland

Funnily enough, a similar thing happened to me the other day with Joan Collins in the lift of my apartment building in Los Angeles. I went to shake her hand, and she said, "Oh no, Ozzy, I can't get sick." Mind you, I can understand the worry: I'm a singer, so if I get a cold on the road, shows can get cancelled and livelihoods are at stake. That's why I use cleanser myself every so often when I'm doing promo. Having said that, I've never given anyone a slimer, and if anyone gave one to me, they wouldn't forget about it in a hurry. I mean, how did you even *know* it was lotion on the guy's hand? For all you know he might have just knocked one out under his desk. Personally, I would have said to him, "What's the f***'s *this*?"—then wiped it off on his tie.

Gilberts (Proper Disposal Of)

Dear Dr. Ozzy:
When I clear my throat, is it ever okay to spit? I hate swallowing, even though I know it's harmless.
Glenn, Birmingham

Depends. If you're a professional footballer, it would be rude not to. If on the other hand you're in the middle of a business lunch, and everyone's drinking tea and eating little finger sandwiches, then no, it ain't a very good idea to start coughing up a massive Gilbert.

Golf Balls (Death By)

Dear Dr. Ozzy:
My husband wants to buy a holiday home in a "gated community"
on a golf course, but I'm afraid of being killed by a stray ball. He
says I'm being paranoid. Am I?
Liz, Surrey

You ain't being paranoid. When I lived in Palm Springs,
Gerald Ford used to hit someone with a golf ball just about
every other week. He might have hit *me* for all I know:
I was drinking so much, I wouldn't have noticed anything
smaller than a flying sledgehammer. It became a standing joke
after a while: you weren't a real local until you had a signed
letter from the President, apologising for the shiner on your
forehead. Not that golf balls are harmless, mind you: they're
as hard as rocks and travel at over 100mph—so yeah, they can
kill you if you're unlucky. But you have to be *very* unlucky.

H.

Hair (Self-Removal Of)

Dear Dr. Ozzy:
For over a year I've been literally tearing out my hair. It started at a time
when I was under immense stress, but I haven't stopped. I'm aware that
it can be described as a mental condition—"trichotillomania"—but
I think of it more as an addiction. As someone who's defeated his own
vices, your wisdom would be greatly appreciated.
Eric, York

No-one's ever fucking happy, are they? Half the time I'm
answering questions from blokes who'd swap their right arm
for a few more follicles, and then here you are, ripping them
all out of your own free will. Seriously, though, you should
really talk to someone about this—a shrink or at the very

least your GP—asap. I mean, yeah, you can call it a habit, or an addiction, or whatever, but the bottom line is that you're harming yourself, and that's heavy duty. In fact, I wouldn't be surprised if the rug-tugging was a symptom of some other issues you've got going on, and if you get some treatment now, you'll probably save yourself a lot of trouble and heartache later on. One thing to maybe ask your doc about is a course of "habit reversal training." From what I understand, it doesn't involve any actual medication, but it can be very effective.

Headbanging (Complications Of)

Dear Dr. Ozzy:
Your column has inspired me to go through my old Black Sabbath collection, but now I have severe bruising on my forehead and an intense ringing in my ears. What's wrong with me?
Simon, Perth, Australia

It's called being a headbanger, Simon. When people first started doing it in the early 1970s, working class guys like me had never had a way of expressing themselves before, and they got carried away. One guy headbanged all night at a Motörhead concert with his head *literally* inside a speaker cabinet—it give him a fatal brain hemorrhage. The thing to realise is that headbanging is just like another exercise: the first time you do it, you're really sore the next day. You've just got to start slowly and keep it up, gradually working yer way up to match fitness. So next time, before putting your Black Sabbath records on, try doing 20 headbangs every morning for a few weeks in advance.

That should help.

Dear Dr. Ozzy,
I'm 19 years old and have rheumatoid arthritis and ankylosing spondylitis (the same back disease that Mick Mars from Mötley

Crüe has). I love headbanging, but can barely move when the adrenaline wears off. Any tips for muscle pain relief?
Karl, USA

I really hate to say this, but why don't you hold back on the headbanging for a bit? I mean, I know Mick, and I know how painful that condition can be. You've got to accommodate what your body can do. People can enjoy music in all kinds of different ways. What amazes me is that I often get deaf people coming to my gigs: they can't hear the lyrics, but they can get into the rhythm. So my advice to you is to keep going to the shows, but get into the vibe in a way that doesn't involve the mosh pit. It ain't worth the agony, man, and I certainly wouldn't recommend popping any heavy-duty pain pills—unless your doctor says you should—as they can be horrendously addictive.

Head Cold (Flying With)

Dear Dr. Ozzy:
The other day I flew to a conference with a "head cold," thinking the change in pressure might clear out my ears. Instead it felt as though my brain was about to explode, and when we finally landed—after what seemed like years—I was deaf on one side (still am). Help...
Lisa, Reading

This ain't much use to you now, Lisa, but you should *never* fly with a really bad head cold, 'cos you can burst your eardrums. So, in the future, do the opposite of what you did. Rent a car, take a boat—swim, if you have to. *But don't get on a plane.* I've heard that you also can buy these plug things that help regulate the pressure, but the trouble is, you've gotta trust yourself to be able to use them properly, and personally I have trouble getting my telly to work, never mind trying to put some microscopic shield in my ear. In the meantime, you need to get checked out by a doc, 'cos you might have done yourself some damage. It's too important to wait and see if it heals by itself.

Hernia (Lump Caused By)

Dear Dr. Ozzy:
I have a hiatus hernia which I've been treating for a few years with Gaviscon tablets, without much improvement. What really bothers me, however, is the lump—a small, circular ball on my navel. Any ideas on how to get rid of this unsightly bulge?
"Mike," Harrow

A friend of mine had the same thing, and unfortunately you can't just tap it a couple of times with a hammer to pop it back in—you need surgery. But this is something you *have* to get checked out by your doc, 'cos it might be more (or less) complicated than you think.

I.

Insect Bites

Dear Dr. Ozzy:
On Tuesday I was cutting bushes in my yard when I accidentally made contact with a bee's nest and was attacked. I only got stung once before I dove into my pool. Two days later, my leg is twice the size it once was. What's wrong with me?
Chris, Danvers, Massachusetts

I once had a keyboard player who had to call for an ambulance if he got stung by a bee. The fact is, some people are a lot more allergic to stings than others, and it sounds like you're having a very nasty reaction. Get it seen to immediately. Hop to the ER if necessary.

J.

Jimmy Legs (A.K.A. Restless Legs)

Dear Dr. Ozzy:
*I suffer from "Jimmy legs," also known as restless leg syndrome.
My legs shake and move about in the night, and it's driving my wife
mad. Any ideas how I can put a stop to this?*
Mick, West Midlands

I have exactly the same problem—and so does my wife,
Sharon. We're like pair of pneumatic drills, jiggling and
wobbling away under the sheets, making the floorboards rattle.
My leg has a mind of its own. It goes all over the place. Even
when I'm sitting down on the sofa, it's bouncing around like
I'm in the back of a rickshaw on a bumpy road. It's one of the
reasons why I can't stay still for more than a few minutes. In
terms of treatment, you can get medication for Jimmy legs, but
it's a form of benzodiazepine—the same thing as Valium—and
I spent decades trying to get off that shit, and I don't want to
go back to it. Maybe it's something you could try, if you don't
have a history with that drug. Personally, I've decided to live
with the condition. I mean, it's not like it's painful. It's just
irritating—and it wears out the bed springs pretty quick.

DR. OZZY'S SURGERY NOTICEBOARD

The Battle of Bouncing Knee

◆ I always crap myself when a real doctor writes to me,
'cos I think I'm about to get a bollocking. Most of the
time, though, they just have a helpful suggestion. For
example, Dr. Geoff, a retired GP from St. Ives, sent me
an e-mail to say that "small doses of anti–parkinsonian
drugs such as Pramipexole [Mirapexin]" can help cure

> your restless legs (you should ALWAYS talk to your
> own GP before trying ANY kind of treatment). Mean-
> while, other readers said that mineral salts, magnesium,
> Crampex tablets, and putting a tablet of toilet soap
> under the bed sheets can do some good. They also say
> you should avoid peppermint, mouthwash, and raspber-
> ries. How anyone could prove that is beyond me.

Dear Dr. Ozzy:
Thanks to a suggestion by one of your readers the other week,
I've been prescribed an anti-parkinsonian drug for my restless leg
syndrome—but when I looked online, I found that the side-effects
might include "intense urges to gamble" and "increased sexual
urges (hypersexuality)." Should I throw the pills in the bin?
David, Buckinghamshire
    . . . and you're *worried* about this? The label might as well say,
"side-effects including having a good time." In all seriousness,
though—there's no point in curing your restless legs only to
blow your life savings in Las Vegas on blackjack and hookers.
Talk to your GP.

K.

King's Speech Technique (Stuttering)

Dear Dr. Ozzy:
As a self-confessed stutterer, have you ever gone through any of the
treatments shown in the film **The King's Speech,** *like putting*
marbles in your mouth, or reciting Shakespeare while wearing
headphones? Do you think a stutter can be cured?
Kim, Santa Barbara, California
    I don't know if a stutter can be cured, but I can tell you how
to get one—drink and do drugs for 40 years. Believe me, getting

to end of a single sentence is a major achievement when you're on your second bottle of cognac and third speedball before breakfast. To answer the first part of your question, though: no, I've never had speech lessons—although I did once get hypnotised by Paul McKenna when I was trying to change my lifestyle. The trouble was, I was blasted at the time, so it's hard to say if I was hypnotised, or if I just passed out, which was a daily occurrence in those days. As for my stutter, it's been a lot better since I sobered up, and I've realised that it's usually brought on by anxiety. When I'm nervous about something, my mind spins faster than my mouth can catch up, so I end up sounding like a World War II machine gun. By taking a deep breath and slowing down a bit, I can usually keep it under control.

L.

Lead (Poisoning)

Dear Dr. Ozzy:
I'm currently renovating my family's Georgian townhouse and have just come across a government leaflet about lead paint. Now I'm terrified that every little thing I do will create poisonous dust that will brain-damage my toddler and pregnant wife. Please help.
Ryan, Edinburgh

A lot of people might not take this kind of thing very seriously, but I had a cousin who was an industrial painter, and he got asbestosis. So if I were you, I'd be wearing a rubber suit and a gas mask in the house. I mean, yeah, people my age grew up eating more lead paint chips than they did French fries, but that doesn't make it any less dangerous. Kids also used to ride in cars without seatbelts while their parents smoked themselves blue in the face with the windows closed: it doesn't mean we should do it *now*. Call your local council, ask them what the right procedure is, and follow it. Meanwhile, if you've already started to sand the woodwork, send your wife and toddler to the in-laws until the job's all done and you've been given the all-clear by a qualified inspector.

DR. OZZY'S SURGERY NOTICEBOARD

Heavy Metal Madness

◆ Tristan Olivier from the Lead Paint Safety Association tells me that local councils might not be much help when it comes to advice on handling toxic dust in old houses (see Ryan from Edinburgh, above). "Given the extent to which childhood lead exposure is linked to reduced IQ, learning and behaviour problems, this is probably the biggest, least known and worst addressed public health issue in the UK," he says. For more info, visit the LPSA's website, at www.lipsa.org.uk.

Legs (Sleepy)

Dear Dr. Ozzy,
My leg keeps "falling asleep" without any warning. Does this mean I have poor circulation?
Lauren, Sheffield

One time, I got drunk, badly drunk—on cognac—and went to sleep in the wrong position, and when I woke up my leg felt like it wasn't even there any more. It was just this useless lump attached to my thigh. At first I didn't think it was a problem… but it went on for *three months*. I went to my doc, and he told me—seriously—that he might have to chop it off. I said to him, "I'm a rock 'n' roll star! I can't hobble around the stage with a wooden leg, singing 'Iron Man'!" Eventually, another doctor took a look at and said that it was more likely caused by my alcoholism. So if you're a heavy drinker, I'd recommend cutting down, or giving up entirely. Otherwise, make sure you don't sit in the same position for a long time. And if you go and see a doctor, remember: if he ever starts using phrases like "electric saw" and "operating table," there ain't nothing stopping you from getting a second opinion. I'm certainly fucking glad I did.

M.

Mourning

Dear Dr. Ozzy:
My wife died in January. I've been having counselling for the last six months but it's very lonely with just me and my two Bedlington terriers. I feel as though I have so much free time and need to fill it. Can you offer any advice on coping with grief?
David, London

The thing I realised when I lost someone who was very close to me—my ex-guitarist Randy Rhoads—is that no-one can ever really prepare you for coping with sudden death. You're pretty much on your own. What you've got to come to terms with is that grief is simply a natural process, and that everyone goes through it at some point in their life. The best thing you can do is join a counselling group, or at least find *someone* you can talk to about it—which it sounds like you're already doing. Having said that, of course, I didn't take any of that advice when Randy died. I locked the grief away, so it manifested itself in other ways, like drugs and alcohol. The trouble was, when I was kid, anyone who went to therapy was one step away from the funny farm. I know better now. I suppose another thing you've gotta accept is that you never *fully* get over the death of someone who's been that close to you. I mean, even today, when I'm on stage playing any of the songs from my two albums with Randy, it's as though he's right there at my side. But it's a good feeling now, not a bad one.

Dear Dr. Ozzy:
I keep suffering terrible anxiety attacks. It started when my uncle—who was like a dad to me—died in his sleep from a random cardiac arrest (I never met my real dad until I was 13). I've been to psychologists, but all they tell me is that if I realise I'm not going to die, the panic will go away. That's bullshit, because I know I won't die... but I still feel like I'm about to blow up inside. Please help...
Don (17 years old), Texas, USA

Sounds to me like grief, Don. People don't take grief seriously enough, because the loss of someone, or even some*thing*, can be very hard to get over. It sounds crazy, but when I was in rehab, I had to attend "grief groups" for the loss of drugs and alcohol in my life. I thought it was stupid at first—especially when I met a guy in there who was sobbing about his recently departed cat—but I soon discovered that grief can mess you up, badly. I wouldn't be surprised if that's what's causing your panic attacks. Your body is overloaded with emotion. So my recommendation would be that you get on the internet and find your own local grief group. It's a lot healthier than going to your GP for a bottle of Valium: that'll just fix one problem and start five others.

N.

Napping (Guidelines Regarding)

Dear Dr. Ozzy:
What's the ideal length for an afternoon nap? My friends swear by them, but every time I doze off during the day I wake up in a terrible mood with a splitting headache.
Ross, Aberdeen

I never used to understand naps. When I was a kid, I'd see my old man dozing off in his favourite chair and think, "You went to bed last night, why d'you need to sleep *now*?" But as I got older myself, I began to understand. For me, the point of a nap isn't about sleep, it's just about getting some "quiet time," so you can recharge. It's a break from all the craziness of modern life. So if you find yourself waking up from a nap feeling like a dog's arsehole, my advice would be, try just giving yourself twenty or thirty chilled-out minutes by yourself instead. Read, do some stretching exercises, or go out for a walk.

Nightmares (Prevention Of)

Dear Dr. Ozzy:
What can I do before I go to bed to prevent bad dreams?
William, Alnwick

Funnily enough, one of the few things I've never had a problem with is nightmares. Every so often I'll have a really *confusing* dream—but never one where a zombie Ryan Seacrest is shooting blood from his eyeballs and trying to cut out my liver with rusty steak knife. Mind you, I didn't dream at all for about 40 years, because I'd never go to bed—the only rest I got was when I blacked out once every three or four days. One time, when I was on tour in America with Mötley Crüe, I blacked out in the central reservation of a twelve-lane freeway (I'd been trying to find somewhere to take a piss). In fact, *waking up* was always the biggest nightmare for me. Not that I'd recommend my former lifestyle as a way to avoid bad dreams. Instead, try thinking about something that makes you feel really good before you shut your eyes. Or have a nice cup of tea—but nothing too stimulating (ie, black coffee). And whatever you do, avoid sleeping pills at all costs, or you might end up with a worse problem than the one you started with.

Nightsweats

Dear Dr. Ozzy:
Almost every night I wake up in the early hours drenched in sweat. It's disgusting—the sheets are soaked through. I've tried to turn up the air conditioning, but to no effect. What's causing this, and how do I stop it from happening?
Olivia, New York

Could be nylon sheets. Those things make me sweat like I'm on Death Row. I can't have 'em near me. Same with feathers, which mess my chest up, and sleeping bags, which are one step removed from being buried alive. If it ain't your sheets, it could be what you're wearing, or it could be an allergy—or the side-effect of some medication you're taking. If I were you, I'd try something different every night, and try and solve it that way.

DR. OZZY'S SURGERY NOTICEBOARD

Wet Dreams

◆ It's amazing how many people wake up in the morning feeling sweatier than one of Jabba the Hut's armpit. One reader, Lisa, wrote to me: "I suffered night sweats for 15 years before a gynaecologist did a blood test and diagnosed that I had next to no oestrogen. Although I wasn't menopausal or pre-menopausal, I was having the same kind of symptoms. Now I take a daily supplement and my life has changed utterly." Meanwhile, Gabrielle in London reckoned she'd solved the problem with a silk-filled duvet, while a GP from Scotland—he didn't want to give his name, funnily enough—said a bad case of the sweats might be a symptom of something called

> "polymyalgia rheumatica." I'm told that means "pain in many muscles" in Greek. Sounds like one of my mid-1980s hangovers.

Nipples (Unusual)

Dear Dr. Ozzy:
Like Francisco Scaramanga in **The Man with the Golden Gun,** *I have a third nipple. Should I be worried?*
Gary, Dorset
    Only if it starts talking to you.

O.

Obscene Language (Excessive Use Of)

Dear Dr. Ozzy:
I've become addicted to swearing. It started two years ago, and basically I swear in nearly every sentence now, even in front of my parents at school. I've tried to stop but can't. I think I must have Tourette's syndrome. What should I do?
Ben, Cheshire
    Swearwords are weird, aren't they? I mean, the American word "schmuck"—which pretty much no-one finds offensive—apparently comes from the Yiddish word "shmok," which is a very rude term for a bloke's Upstanding Citizen. It's as bad as calling someone the C-word. Then there's the English word "bollocks"—which I *love*—which used to be slang for a Vicar, or so I've been told (although in the old days a more common way of spelling it was "Ballocks"). People just *decide* which words they want to get upset about, basically. So my advice to you, Ben, is to carry on swearing as much as you like: just do it in a foreign language. That way you won't get into any trouble.

P.

Pain (Management Of)

Dear Dr. Ozzy:
A few weeks ago, while in a New York hotel room, I accidently stepped on the door stop. The pain was intense. Now, three weeks later, it hurts when I walk. I think I might have broken something in my foot. What's your expert medical opinion?
Mark, Rancho Santa Fe, California

There's an easy to fix to this one, Mark: try playing football. You'll know if it's broken after that.

Dear Dr. Ozzy:
I have just had a gallbladder operation and, frankly, I feel bloody awful. Given the many medical disasters you've recovered from during your lifetime, what are your rehabilitation tips?
Hec, Glasgow

Two words: baby steps. You've just had someone rip open your stomach with a knife, so you can't expect to be starring in *Riverdance* any time soon. Having said that, I wasn't exactly very patient after I fell off my quad bike and ended up in a coma for eight days. As soon as I woke up, I tried to check myself out. Hospitals aren't very nice places to be, in my opinion—if only for the fact that there's fuck all to do in there. But I've now learned that you've gotta go easy on yourself as much as you can. Trust me: if you're too impatient, you're only gonna end slowing down your recovery in the long term.

Parents (Living With)

Dear Dr. Ozzy:
Okay, I'm just going to come out and say it: I'm 40 years old, between jobs, and single. How bad is it if I move back in with my

parents, who have plenty of room at home? I'm not relishing the
thought, but it would save money while I get my life together.
Robert, Pontefract, West Yorks

It sounds like you're trying to live your life by other people's
rules. If you like your parents, and they don't mind you in
their house, then move in. If you were Italian, you wouldn't
even think twice about it—most guys over there live with
their mothers until they get hitched, no matter how long it
takes. I realise people might not be so cool with that kind
of thing in West Yorkshire, but it's a lot fucking better than
being so broke you can't afford to eat, never mind pay for
dates. Just do what you've gotta do, man.

Phobias (Pigeons, Etc.)

Dear Dr. Ozzy:
Every time I get on a plane, I convince myself that I'm going to die.
It's reached the point where I'm starting to make excuses at work to
avoid travelling overseas. Please help!
Liz, Buckinghamshire

Flying can be deadly. For example, I was on a plane once to
America and the bloke next to me started to make funny noises
while eating his nuts. Next thing I knew, I was sitting next to a
corpse. The worst thing was having to press the little buzzer to
call for a flight attendant, and then explain why a bloke who'd
been alive a few minutes earlier was suddenly face down on his
tray table. For a moment, I thought they'd send out Columbo
to meet me when I landed at JFK. In the end they put a blanket
over him and moved me to a seat in first class with champagne.
I only mention this story because I'm told that having someone
drop dead next to you is probably more likely than your plane
falling out of the sky. In fact, they say you're more likely to die
in a car crash on the way to the airport than you are to die in a
plane crash. But not many people lie awake at night, worrying

about the drive to Heathrow. Try reminding yourself of that next time you have to fly somewhere. It might calm you down.

Dear Dr. Ozzy,
My friend has a rare phobia: she's terrified of pigeons. Is there a cure?
Anna, Finland

I ain't got a clue, but if your friend lives in Finland, how many pigeons does she come across on a daily basis? I mean, if she lived in the middle of Trafalgar Square, it might be a problem. It's not like the Finns eat pigeons, either: all they have over there is reindeer burgers, reindeer ice cream, and reindeer stew. Tell her to picture a sparrow and relax.

Dear Dr. Ozzy:
I'm terrified of butterflies. Is this is a common phobia? And what should I do now that the summer is approaching, and my room will soon become infested with the horrible things?
Lola, Irish Republic

I had no idea it was possible to get so upset about butterflies. I mean, what else are you scared of? Rainbows, puppies, and sunny days? Personally, the only creatures I really can't stand are rats. If I see one, I freak, big time. But what can you do? You can't walk around all day in HAZMAT suit with a bag over your head on the off-chance you might come across one. Having said that, it's pretty easy to stay out of the way of rats, but it might be a bit harder with butterflies. If it's causing you a lot of anxiety, talk to your GP. Maybe he'll be able to sign you up for some kind of desensitization therapy.

Q.

Quinquaud's Decalvans Folliculitis*

---

*I'm fucked if I know what this is, apart from the fact it begins with the letter "Q."

R.

Rabies (Suspected)

Dear Dear Ozzy:
How can I tell if I've got rabies? The reason I ask is because I was bitten by a stray dog while on holiday in Turkey, and now I'm worried it might have given me a terrible disease.
Denise, Portsmouth

I thought I'd caught rabies after eating that bat in Des Moines, Iowa. The injections they gave me were horrendous: one in each arm, one in each arse cheek, one in each thigh. Then you've got to rub the stuff like crazy to make sure it spreads over the muscle. It's like an oil, very dense—you can feel it trickling around inside you. It's the safest thing to do, and I'm sure the treatments have improved since 1982, but it ain't very nice. Personally, I gave up halfway through. I said to Sharon, "If I start barking, we can start up again."

DR. OZZY'S SURGERY NOTICEBOARD

Going Batty

◆ According to Bernard in London, *anyone* who gets bitten by a stray animal in a faraway country like Turkey should immediately go and see a doctor—not wait until they start howling at the moon—'cos it could be "a life and death matter." Even though I didn't finish my own rabies treatment in 1982 after eating a bat's head on stage, Bernard says the injections I had in hospital later that night might very well have saved my life.

S.

Sleeping Pills

Dear Dr. Ozzy:
*I can't stop taking sleeping pills—this has been going on for about
five years now. I'm out of work, and at a loss what to do. Help.*
Yoshizawa, Japan

I'm convinced that once you start relying on sleeping pills,
it damages your sleeping pattern forever. A lot of sleeping pills
are made from benzodiazepine, which is the same family as
Valium—very addictive stuff. When I finally got off it after 25
years, it was the worst withdrawal I ever had from anything.
The way I stopped was by switching my sleeping medication to
an anti-depressant called trazodone, and I recommend that you
talk to your doctor over there in Japan about doing something
similar. The secret is to go very slowly: there's no hurry. I also
tried using a non-benzodiazepine sleeping pill, Ambien—or
zolpidem—but it was the worst. My short-term memory got
so bad I didn't even know what time of day it was (see page 3).
Mind you, I wasn't just taking the regular dosage. I built up
such a tolerance, I was popping the fucking things like M&M's.

Sleepwalking

Dear Dr. Ozzy,
*I keep waking up in my next-door neighbour's front garden. I live
alone, so either someone is coming into my house in the middle of
the night and carrying me there, or I'm sleep-walking. Have you
ever heard of this? What can I do about it?*
Jane, Bradford

I'm always pottering about in the middle of the night, fast
asleep. I was in a B&B one time, and I sleep-walked into the

wrong room, got into bed, and carried on with my whatever dream I was having. Then this big hairy bloke climbs between the sheets with me. I wake up and go, "What are *you* doing here?" He takes one look at me, screams, claps his hands over his wedding tackle, and goes, "WHAT THE FUCK ARE *YOU* DOING HERE?" Sadly, there ain't no cure for sleep-walking, as far as I know. But it's not always a bad thing. A few years ago, for example, I was sleep-walking around my house in Buckinghamshire, when I walked smack into a burglar. If that doesn't wake you up, nothing will. I almost caught the guy, too. I put him in a headlock for about five minutes, but didn't have any handcuffs or anything, so in the end I thought, fuck it, and threw him out of the window...and he hobbled off across the field with about $3 million worth of Sharon's jewelery in a plastic bag. Still, looking on the bright side, if I hadn't been sleep-walking, I would never have met a real-life diamond thief.

Snoring

Dear Dr. Ozzy:

Is a marriage automatically dead if the two parties start using separate bedrooms? I ask because my wife has developed a snore loud enough to wake the mummies in Egypt, and I can't sleep next to her without large and unwise doses of medication.

Viv, Hull

No, relax, your marriage ain't over. I know quite a few people with very healthy relationships who sleep in different rooms, 'cos they don't want to listen to a human chainsaw next to them when they're trying to get some shut-eye. I mean, if you're the first one to drop off, it ain't a problem— and it's easy to get offended when your other half starts complaining—but for the poor sod who's still awake, it's excruciating. Having said all that, you might want to look into some anti-snoring gizmos before taking the separate-bedroom option. If you get on the internet you can find all kinds of things, from mouthpieces to clothes pegs and special pillows. Why not give one of 'em a try?

T.

Transvestism

Dear Dr. Ozzy:
For years I've fantasised about what it would be like to be a woman—to the extent where I've started to shop for girls' clothing and wear my wife's underwear when she's away on business. How can I explain this to her, or is that a terrible idea?
David, Watford

Okay, so you've got two choices, David: pluck up the courage to tell her now, or get caught later. It's really that simple. As much as you think you can hide this forever, it's obviously such a big part of who you are, I guarantee that one day you'll have a couple of drinks, put a frock on, and the missus will come home early and hit the roof. That's gonna be a much harder conversation than if you bring it up gently at your own pace. And—who knows?—your wife might not even care. I mean, here in Los Angeles, there's a whole society for cross-dressers. They're all builders and postmen and delivery boys or whatever. They get dressed up in their fishnets, go out clubbing, come home, then go back to work the next day in their overalls like nothing happened.

Tubs (Hot Ones)

Dear Dr. Ozzy:
My husband has bought a "hot tub" and put it in our back garden, but I refuse to get in it, because I've heard horror stories about the

water becoming a breeding-ground for germs. He says I'm worrying too much, and spends half of the weekend in there. What's your opinion?
Betty, Portsmouth

You're both right. There's nothing better than being outdoors in a hot tub on a crisp October evening, drinking a nice glass of something cold. At the same time, if you don't maintain a hot tub properly, it can turn into a swamp, with algae and frogs and fuck-knows-what-else floating around in there. I mean, even though it's shiny and blue, with pressure jets and mood lighting, a hot tub is still basically just a big boiling cauldron of chemicals. The worst is when you have a party and a bunch of hairy blokes climb in there, all burping and farting and blowing their noses. That grosses me out, that does. Another thing with hot tubs: you've gotta watch the heat. I used to get blasted on cocaine, feel my heart begin to pound, then try to calm down by jumping into 900-degree water. One time, I swear my head almost *exploded*. But if your husband cleans his new toy regularly—tell him to sign up for a weekly maintenance service—there's no reason not to take a dip. You never know, it might improve your love life.

U.

Urination (Nervous Pisser Syndrome)

Dear Dr. Ozzy:
If I'm standing next to another man at a public urinal, I can't pee. Even if I'm desperate to go—not a drop. I once queued up for 20 minutes at a rock concert to use the loo, and then had to walk away, because I was wedged between two big blokes. I've never known any of my friends to have the same problem. What's wrong with me?
Terry, Essex

Let me ask you a question, Terry: when this happens, are you *absolutely sure* you need to pee? I mean, when I need to relieve myself, there ain't no choice about it. I don't care if the Coldstream Guards are standing next to me, whatever's inside is coming out. So my advice is to wait until you're more desperate to go. Or see a shrink: it might be anxiety.

DR. OZZY'S SURGERY NOTICEBOARD

"Performance" Anxiety

◆ Important news from Ray in Suffolk: "According to a study of public urinal usage in America, 'flow start' was delayed by an average of 20 seconds when two blokes were standing right next to each other—as opposed to a solo effort." So poor old Terry in Essex obviously ain't suffering alone.

V.

Vaginas (Fishy)

Dear Dr. Ozzy:
I've been told that the best way to prevent unpleasant odour in your private areas is to avoid using soap, only water. This sounds a bit counterintuitive to me. Could it be true?
Tyler (no address given)

It would help to know if you were a guy or a girl. Assuming you own a pair of testicles, whoever gave you this advice obviously wasn't planning on sitting next to you in a hot car any time soon. In general, avoiding soap is never gonna prevent unpleasant odours. The only thing it's gonna prevent is you making any friends—unless you're using a power hose (which I obviously don't recommend). If you're a member of the more complicated sex, on the other hand, my wife tells me that you do actually need to be very careful when it comes to soap and your sensitive areas, especially if you like lathering yourself up with the heavily scented grandma-type stuff. Bear in mind, though: the Prince of Darkness ain't exactly a world-authority on female anatomy. If you're really concerned about it, get yourself an appointment with a gynaecologist.

Vertigo

Dear Dr. Ozzy:
I suffer from vertigo. What can I do to cure it?
Nilay, Istanbul, Turkey

I thought I had vertigo for 40 years. I went to the doctor and he said, "Mr. Osbourne, the problem—as far as I can tell—is that you're drunk. Very drunk." So my prescription for you is to go to bed for 24 hours, drink *nothing*—apart from water—then get up and walk around in circles for a bit. If you're still feeling dizzy, you might have a problem.

W.

Wax (Big Lumps Of)

Dear Dr. Ozzy,
I used a cotton wool bud to clean out my ears the other day and dislodged some wax—now I'm half-deaf. Is there an easy way to get rid of the wax without going to the doctor's?
Lucy, Carlisle

Short answer: no. Don't mess with your ears, man. Go to a real doctor. I remember getting a smack around the head once from Sharon, and her hand clipped the wrong spot and burst my eardrum. I had to get a plug in my ear for ages while it healed. It was like walking around with a cardboard box on my head. Sharon felt terrible. Not as bad as I felt, though. So don't mess around with your ears: they're too important, and too easy to break.

Weird S***

Dear Dr. Ozzy:
If I open my mouth in a certain way, I can fire saliva like it's a water pistol. What should I do?
Christopher, Bristol
Try not opening your mouth. That should fix it.

X.

X-Rays (Dangers Of)

Dear Dr. Ozzy,
Thanks to airport scanners, the new 3-D imaging equipment in my dentist's office, and cosmic radiation from long-haul flights, I'm worried that I'm turning into a one-man Chernobyl. Should I try to cut down on all this radiation exposure?
Brad, Somerset
You're talking to someone who's been flying on a weekly basis since the late 1960s. I probably give off more cosmic radiation than Halley's fucking Comet—and that's before adding in all the airport scans I've had, or the thousands of visits to my dentist. Having said that, by far the longest exposure I ever had to an X-ray was for the cover of one my albums, *Down to Earth*. The bloke in charge of the artwork had to shout directions to me through a four-foot brick wall, 'cos he was so scared of getting cancer. At that point in my life, though, getting zapped with death-rays was probably the safest thing I'd done all year. These days, radiation is just a fact

of life, so there's no point in letting it drive you nuts. I mean, yeah, it's a pain in the arse going through airport security, but your chances of getting sick have gotta be close to zero. And what's the alternative? Getting blasted out of the sky at 37,000 feet? I'll take the X-ray, thanks.

Y.

Yawning (Side-Effects)

Dear Dr. Ozzy:
Whenever I yawn, my eyes water—to the point where it looks like I'm about to cry. How can I stop this?
Lex, Surrey

Easy: stop doing things that make you yawn. Have you tried skydiving?

Z.

Zoning Out (Driving)

Dear Dr. Ozzy:
When driving long distances, what's the best way to stay awake at the wheel? I've tried keeping the window open, but I still find my eyes glassing over and having to take a break.
Raj, Birmingham

I knew some roadies in the 1970s who could drive from Land's End to John O'Groats and back ten times thanks to the rocket powder they were putting up their noses on a daily basis. But the truth is, driving when you're high is as stupid as driving when you're exhausted. Either way, you could end up killing yourself—or worse, someone else. If you want to cover a lot of miles without stopping, get a co-driver. Or better yet, take the train.

Dr. Ozzy's Trivia Quiz: Doctor! Doctor!

Find the answers—and tote up your score—on page 263

1. Which drug was the Harold "Dr. Death" Shipman addicted to?
   a) Pethidine (known as Demerol in the U.S.)
   b) Codeine
   c) Vicodin (hydrocodone/paracetamol)

2. A woman in England recently sued her doctor for giving her *what*?
   a) Two "leg-buckling" orgasms within 90 seconds of each other
   b) Oral herpes
   c) A slap in the face to wake her up

3. A dentist in North Carolina, USA, was accused of using a syringe to inject this into his patients' mouths:
   a) LSD
   b) His own semen
   c) A home-made numbing gel made from dog's liver

4. To advertise a new technique he'd invented, a British GP performed what surgery on himself?
   a) Tendon repair
   b) Kneecap replacement
   c) Vasectomy

5. A survey of GPs in America found that 73 per cent of them had...

   a) Been turned on by a patient
   b) Made sure that a rude patient spent longer in the waiting room
   c) Done things to patients that weren't necessary, just to look better in court if they were sued

Genetics Explained...
Sort Of

7

Before Reading, Apply Ice-Pack to Brain

When I got a call one morning from an editor at *The Sunday Times* in London telling me that some scientists wanted to "sequence my genome," I didn't know what to say. Not 'cos I was surprised—*nothing* could surprise me any more when it comes to the crazy shit that happens in my life—I just didn't understand what the fuck he was talking about. The only "genome" I'd ever heard of was the kind you find down the bottom of the garden with a white beard and a pointy red hat.

"You *what*?" I said. "A gnome?"

"No, a *gee-nome*," laughed the guy on the phone. "Basically all your genes and the bits in between, mapped out on a computer. The company that arranges it—and hires the scientists to analyse the results—is called Knome, Inc. It was founded by a top Harvard professor."

To be honest with you, I didn't like the sound of it. I'm a rock star, not Brain of Britain. And even if they did the test, how would I know what it said? The only Gene I know

anything about is the one in Kiss. Still, it's not every day someone wants to unravel your DNA—so I asked if anyone else
had done the same thing. "Only about 200 people, because
the technology is so expensive," said the editor (my assistant
Tony was taking notes). "The first human genome they ever
sequenced was in 1990, but they didn't get the final results
until more than a decade later in 2003. It cost $3 billion."

"Well that rules it out then," I said. "I ain't got $3 billion."

"Prices have come down," he replied. "Besides, in your
case, Knome say they can raise the cash from other people.
They'll provide you with your entire genome on a USB drive
the size of a Zippo lighter. Then they'll go through the results
with you in person, line by line."

I still didn't get it. Why spend the money on *me* when
they could do someone like Stephen Hawking? "Look,"
said the editor, "you've said it yourself: you're a *medical miracle*. You went on a drink and drugs bender for 40 years.
You broke your neck on a quad bike. You died twice in a
chemically induced coma. You walked away from your tour
bus without a scratch after it was hit by a plane. Your immune
system was so compromised by your lifestyle, you got a positive HIV test for 24 hours, until they proved it was wrong.
And yet here you are, alive and well and living in Buckinghamshire."

"So the test can *really* tell me why I'm still here?" I asked.

"It won't tell you everything—scientists still have a lot more
work to do before they understand how genes work. But it
might help make sense of a lot of things. It will also be able to
tell if anything in your genes is linked to, say, Alzheimer's disease. But you're in your sixties, so anything *really* scary in your
DNA would have probably killed you a long time ago, along
with that line of ants you once snorted with Mötley Crüe."

"What if they find a kind of new gene? Will I get a disease
named after me?"

"Possibly."

That was enough for me. "Okay then," I said. "I'll do it."

A few weeks later, a medic came to my house in Chalfont St. Peter to take my blood. I was having a day off from my world tour at the time—and to be honest with you, I was so knack-ered, I began to wonder what the fuck I was doing. I mean, it's not a great feeling, being a human petri-dish. Then again, I was curious. Given the swimming pools of booze I've guzzled over the years—not to mention all the cocaine, morphine, sleeping pills, cough syrup, LSD, Rohypnol... you name it—there's really no plausible medical reason why I should still be alive. Maybe my DNA could say why.

As soon as the guy in the white coat was done taking his sample, he put the test tube in an envelope and told me he was going to send it off to a lab in New Jersey. "First they'll extract the DNA, then they'll process it at a place called Cofactor Genomics in St. Louis, Missouri," he said (again, Tony was scribbling away, 'cos I knew I'd never remember any of this later).

"At Cofactor," the medic went on, "they use a machine that costs almost half a million quid to read your DNA and 'sequence' your genes, then they'll download the whole thing onto a hard drive and post it back to Knome. After that, researchers will go through it all with a fine-tooth comb, to see what your genes have to say about you. Start to finish, the whole thing should take about 13 weeks. Not bad, when the first one took 13 years."

"Next year it'll probably take 13 fucking minutes," I said. The guy just smiled nervously. Then he cleared off. The next day I went back to my tour and put it all out of my mind.

It was three months later when I finally got a call saying they were gonna send over another bloke—Dr. Nathan—to deliver my results. Sharon couldn't be with me for the

presentation, 'cos of some badly timed meetings in Los Angeles, so she called him up beforehand to make sure he wasn't
going to tell me that my head might explode in 2013, or some
other horrendous news. Strangely enough, though, I wasn't
nervous. Probably 'cos I wasn't expecting to understand a
word of what the guy had to say.

I've since learned that Dr. Nathan—who looks way too
young to have so many letters after his name—is an expert
in "primate DNA." And I have to say, I felt pretty primi-
tive when I was listening to him: it was like he'd swallowed
Google for breakfast, then had a couple of encyclopaedias for
lunch. The first thing he did was give me a silver box with
Latin written on the lid ("It means 'Know Thyself,'" he told
me, "it's from the Temple of Apollo"). When I opened it up,
there was one of those little USB drive things inside. The doc
took it out, popped it into his laptop, and the screen filled up
with about ten billion numbers and letters...line after line
after line after line of 'em. It would have taken me ten years
to read one page. "Well, there it is," said Dr. Nathan, proudly.
"Your genome."

"Okay," I said. "But what the fuck does it *mean*?"

"Well, it shows you pretty much all of the 20,000 to 25,000
genes in your body," he explained. "Better than that, it tells
you *what order* they're put together, then it cross-checks that
with other people's genomes. Now, most people's genomes are
very similar, because we're all from the same species, right?
But there are all kinds of tiny differences that let you see what
kind of traits you have, or what diseases you might get."

The craziest thing Dr. Nathan told me is that we all have
the Huntington's gene—it's if you're *missing* any genes that
you're in big trouble—but only people with certain types will
ever come down with the disease. Another thing that blew
me away is how much they already know about the genes
involved in things like Huntington's: they know so much, in

fact, even if you *don't* have the disease, your DNA can tell you straight up whether or not you're likely to pass it on to your kids. That's pretty heavy-duty stuff, and I can see why a lot of people might not want to know. Personally, I'm not that bothered. I've already had all my kids, so it's too late to worry now. And even if my DNA told me that I was a goner, I could still get run over by a truck tomorrow—or poisoned by a radioactive duck turd—long before whatever it was they found in my genome had a chance to kill me. And we all have to die of *something*. At least if you know what's coming, you might get a chance to put it off for a while.

The one thing Dr. Nathan told me to remember about all this genome stuff is that it's still only in its very early days. Until everyone on the planet has had the test done—and the results are fed into some megacomputer, along with everyone's medical files—it'll be more for scientists and rich nerds than anything else. As the doc put it: "Looking at someone's genome today is a bit like trying watch colour TV on a black-and-white set."

Even on a black-and-white set, though, you can still see a picture—and Dr. Nathan had some pretty far-out things to tell me. The first big piece of news is that I have a famous cousin I never knew about: Stephen Colbert, the American funny guy. "You both have mitochondrial DNA passed down from your mothers in 'Haplogroup-T,'" he said.

"Haplo... *what*?"

"Put it this way: Less than 3 per cent of people from European descent are in this group," he said. "Colbert hasn't had his full genome sequenced but he did have that part of his DNA tested—for a second time, actually—just a few months ago, which is how we know. In the grand scheme of things, you're close cousins. Your mothers' lines go back to a pair of sisters a few thousand years ago. Our best guess is that they were living in the area of the Black Sea at the time. Most randomly chosen people would have to go back about 90,000 years to find a common ancestor."

There's only one problem with this life-changing revelation, as far as I'm concerned: if the doc hadn't told me, I wouldn't know who the fuck Stephen Colbert is—I've never watched his TV show. From now on, though, I'm going to be his most loyal viewer. I mean, I'm always watching the stuff my wife does on telly, so I should do the same for other family members, I suppose. Having said that: why couldn't they have found out that I'm related to Paul McCartney or John Lennon? Not that I'm short of famous cousins now— thanks to this test, I'm coming down with them. "Your DNA also tested positive for an even smaller part of Haplogroup-T, called Haplogroup-T2," said Dr. Nathan.

Apparently this makes me a distant relation of Henry "Skip" Gates, a big deal Harvard professor and a mate of President Obama's. (This isn't as crazy as it sounds, 'cos the guy was arrested and charged with disorderly conduct not too long ago. That's pretty good evidence of an Osbourne gene, I reckon.) Other members of my extended family include the original Jesse James, the last Russian Tsar (Nicholas II), and even George I of Britain. I'm sure the royals will be over the fucking moon with that piece of information.

A lot of the other stuff in my genome was more reassuring than mind-blowing. For example: I don't have any dodgy genes that are strongly linked to cancer, Huntington's, or Parkinson's (which I thought I had for a long time, before my doctor realised that I suffer from a "Parkinsonian-like tremor"). So maybe I'll get to live as long as my indestructible nan, who made it to the age of 99. They also found nothing in my genes that suggests I'm very likely to get Alzheimer's, which is a relief, given what Sharon's dad went through with that horrendous disease. Another thing Dr. Nathan discovered is that I'm part Neanderthal. That won't come as much of a surprise to the missus—or various police departments around the world. But Dr. Nathan thought it was pretty interesting. "It was only a few months ago that scientists managed to sequence a Neanderthal genome from old bones found in a Croatian cave and found a link with humans," he said. "Previously, it was thought that all modern humans came from Africa about 50,000 to 60,000 years ago. Now we know there was some Neanderthal-human inter-breeding, which is why there's a small part of Neanderthal in your DNA."

All this is news for blokes everywhere, I think: if the Neanderthals could get lucky with human females, there's hope for us all. (One thing which blew my mind is that I have *less* Neanderthal in me than quite a few very brainy people. The professor guy who founded Knome, George Church, has *three times* more caveman in him than I do.)

Speaking of dead relatives, it also turns out that I share some DNA with the people killed in Pompeii when Mount Vesuvius blew its top in AD 79 (scientists took samples from the bodies in the ash, which is how they can tell). That means I'm also probably also descended from some of the survivors. Which makes a lot of sense, I suppose. If any of the Roman Osbournes drank anywhere near as much booze as I used to, they wouldn't have even *felt* the burning lava. They could have just walked it off.

DR. OZZY'S INSANE BUT TRUE STORIES—

How the "Osbourne Identity" Was Unlocked

◆ In July 2010, a "phlebotomist"—whatever the fuck that is—took a sample of my blood and sent it to a lab in New Jersey.

- DNA was taken from my white blood cells, dissolved in a salt solution, and then sent off to Cofactor Genomics in St. Louis, Missouri.
- At Cofactor, my DNA was "chopped up" into 10 to 25 trillion pieces thanks to some heavy-duty shaking. After that, they spelled out all the chemical letters—in precise order—that make me the certifiable nutter I am.
- For the next 16 days, Cofactor used a photocopier-sized machine—which costs more than *three* Ferraris, so I'm told—to "read" my genome 13 times over and put it on a hard drive.
- The hard drive with "me" on it was sent to Knome, Inc., in Cambridge, Massachusetts.
- Knome compared the 6 *billion* letters in my genome with every other genome on the planet—to find why the fuck I'm still alive. Then they put all the findings on a little USB stick thing and presented it to me at home.
- While trying to understand what had just happened... my brain exploded.

Apart from the distant ancestor stuff—which seems more fun than useful, to be honest—Dr. Nathan told me things based on my DNA that only my wife or my personal assistant could ever have known. Trying to get him to say it in English was another matter. "There are some variants in your '*RNASE3*' gene that suggest you're 240 times more likely than other people to have allergies, according to research," he told me, for example.

Now, although those kind of odds are supposed to be quite unreliable—Dr. Nathan said they shouldn't be trusted—they happen to be spot on in my case: I'm allergic to dust mites, and I get bad sinus infections. So who knows? Maybe the Osbourne snot gene might end up helping to find a cure for hay fever. I could think of worse ways to be remembered.

But that was just the beginning of what they found in the nose department when they were poking around in my DNA. "You also have some nonsense variants in nine of your odor receptor genes," said Dr. Nathan.

"Eh?"

"Basically it means you might not be able to smell a few things—which isn't all that unusual, because modern humans don't have to sniff-out their dinner from two miles away, then go and club it to death. As the species has evolved, our sense of smell has become less sensitive."

I couldn't believe what I was hearing: my old man used to claim that he didn't have *any* sense of smell—or very little. We always thought he was taking the mickey. Me and my brother used to take it in turns to fart silently next to him, to try and catch him out. But he never fell for it—so maybe he was telling the truth, after all. Maybe it was all in his genes.

Another thing they found is that my body ain't any good at metabolising coffee. ("You're a slow acetylator of caffeine," is how Dr. Nathan put it—according to Tony's scribbled notes—"because of the way your *NAT2* gene works.") That explains a lot: I like the occasional blast of espresso, but all it takes is one shot, and my eyeballs feel like they're gonna explode and I start shaking enough to register on the Richter scale.

Now I know why.

Bearing in mind what Dr. Nathan said about those odds figures being a bit dodgy, here are some of the other interesting things he told me: I'm 6.13 times more likely than the average person to have alcohol dependency or alcohol cravings (er... yeah); 1.31 times more likely to have a cocaine addiction; and 2.6 times more likely to have hallucinations while taking cannabis (makes sense, although I was usually loaded on so many different things at the same time, it was hard to know what

was doing what). Meanwhile, I scored low on the genes associated with heroin addiction (I was never addicted to street
heroin, 'cos it made me throw up—a terrible waste of booze—
but I did get very addicted to morphine for a long time). I also
scored low for nicotine addiction, which is interesting, 'cos
cigarettes were the first thing I gave up when I got sober.

To be completely honest with you, some of the stuff Dr.
Nathan told me seemed a bit on the bleedin' obvious side. I
mean, if I'd have been the bloke who forked out $3 billion for
the first test, I'm not sure I would have been too impressed
when the doc told me, "Well, Mr Osbourne, Your *PTPN11*
gene is normal-ish—so you don't have Noonan Syndrome."

"What's Noonan Syndrome?" I asked.

"A type of dwarfism."

"So I'm not a dwarf?"

"No."

"Oh. That's a relief then."

And like I said before, there are lot of things they just don't
know yet. For example: Dr. Nathan says I have 300,000 completely new "spellings" in my DNA—"Of course I do, I'm
fucking dyslexic!" I told him—but they don't really know
what that means. "One of those never-seen-before things
we found in your genome was a regulatory segment in your
ADH4 gene, which metabolises alcohol," said Dr. Nathan. "It
could make you more able to break down alcohol than the
average person. Or less able." Given that I used to drink four
bottles of cognac a day, I'm not sure anyone needs a Harvard
scientist to get to the bottom of that particular mystery.

"We also found new disruptions in your *TTN* and *CLTCL1*
genes," the doc went on. "The first one might be associated
with anything from deafness to Parkinsonianism, while we
know that the second one can affect brain chemistry. If you
wanted to find out more about your addictive behaviour, that
might not be a bad place to start."

If anything tells you how far all this stuff has to come, that pretty much sums it up for me: I mean, if there's a gene for addictive behaviour, you'd have thought that mine would be written in pink neon with a ribbon and a bow on top.

Of all the parts of my genome that make up who I am—from my Pompei ancestors to my snotty nose and the fact I'm ready to blast through the ceiling after one cup of coffee—it was the last thing Dr. Nathan told me that really stuck in my mind. "You have two versions of a gene known as *COMT*," he said. "The first is often called the 'warrior variant,' and the second is known as the 'worrier variant.' A lot of people have one or the other—not both." I suppose that makes me both a warrior *and* a worrier.

It reminded me of a time, years and years ago, when I was on holiday in Hawaii with this chick I knew. We were walking along a cliff-edge one day, and when I told her I was afraid of heights, she couldn't believe it.

"I'm being serious," I remember saying. "I'd get vertigo wearing your high heels."

She just burst out laughing. I couldn't work out what was so funny. Eventually, she said, "You don't remember last night, do you? We were walking along this very same cliff and you ripped off your shirt and took a running jump. I don't think you even looked to see if there were any rocks below. Luckily, you hit water. Then you wanted me to jump after you."

Not being insane, she refused.

I always thought it was just the booze and drugs that made me do crazy things like that, even though I've always been a terrible hypochondriac, and in some ways quite an anxious and insecure person. But now I'm thinking it's got more to do with my genes. Being a warrior—the crazy, Alamo-pissing, bat-eating Prince of Darkness—has made me famous. Being a worrier has kept me alive when some of my dearest friends never made it beyond their mid-twenties.

Before Dr. Nathan left, I told him my theory. He frowned, nodded a bit, squinted his eyes. Then he said, "Look, Mr. Osbourne, after studying your history, taking your blood, extracting your genes from the white cells, making them readable, sequencing them, analysing and interpreting the data using some of the most advanced technology available in the world today—and of course comparing your DNA against all the current research in the U.S. National Library of Medicine, not to mention the eighteenth revision of the public human reference genome—I think I can say with a good deal of confidence why you're still alive."

I looked at him.

He looked at me.

"Go on, then," I said. "Spit it out."

"Sharon," he replied.

Dr. Ozzy's Trivia Quiz: Mutant Strains

Find the answers—and tote up your score—on page 263

1. Which of these creatures might have existed in real life years ago—thanks to a far-out genetic mutation?
   a) Hobbits
   b) Unicorns
   c) Dragons

2. What was genetically special about Lakshmi Tatama when she was born in Bihar, India, in 2005?
   a) She had four arms and four legs
   b) She had a conjoined headless twin
   c) She had three heads

3. What do scientsts put in genetically altered salmon to help keep them alive in very cold water?
   a) Antifreeze
   b) Polar bear DNA
   c) Special "alleles" that tell the fish to grow thicker skin

4. Scientists understand genetics because of this garden vegetable:
   a) Carrots
   b) Brussels sprouts
   c) Peas

5. The world's first cloned sheep, Dolly, was named in honour of...
   a) One of the scientists who created her
   b) Dolly Parton's tits
   c) Doncaster Polytechnic

CHAPTER NOTES: BLAME IT ON THE DNA

MAJOR LIFE EVENT	Biting head off winged nocturnal mammal.	Pissing on the Alamo—by accident.	Not being dead.	Drinking four bottles of cognac a day during most of the 1980s.	Being off my fucking rocker most of the time.
GENETIC CAUSE	"COMT": Both variants ("Val158" and "Met158")	A number of genes on Chromosome 10	"Haplogroup-T2"	"ADH4"	"NAT2"
WHAT IT MEANS	I'm a warrior AND a worrier—ie, I act like a lunatic but go to the doc's afterwards.	Finally, it's official: I'm part-Neanderthal.	Some of my distant relatives survived Pompeii in AD 79 (probably).	According to the doc, I have "an unusual variant near one of my alcohol dehydrogenase genes."	My body can't process caffeine.
NOTE TO SELF	Did someone just call me a COMT?	Next time, say, "Sorry Officer, it wasn't me, it was my caveman gene."	Survive Mount Vesuvius, and you can survive anything…even a bollocking from Sharon.	Translation: I'm a natural born pisshead.	Drink more coffee.

Friends & Arseholes

8

For People Who Aren't People *People*

Only two things in life are supposed to be inevitable: death and taxes. Unfortunately that ain't true, 'cos there's something else you'll never be able to avoid unless you live in Antarctica, Siberia, or Northumberland: *people*. They're everywhere. At work. In shops. On your Facebollocks computer thing. And that's a massive problem if you ain't a people person, 'cos you'll end up spending half your life getting into arguments, feeling embarrassed, not knowing what to say, having the piss taken out of you, or, even worse than all that, just being a boring fucker at parties. Luckily, Dr. Ozzy is here to help. Even if your idea of holiday is a month by yourself in a cave, all you have to do is follow the advice in this chapter, and you'll be able to handle anything another human being can throw at you. Just don't expect to *like* them.

Or for them to like you.

Dear Dr. Ozzy:

I hate "bear-hugging" other men, even close friends. How do I avoid it without offending anyone?

Rafael, Windsor

You've got a mouth, so say something. I know some tough-guy types who think it's cool to say hello by getting me in a headlock and wrestling me to the ground—a "buddy slam" they call it over here in California. More like a load of macho bollocks, if you ask me. So if they try it, I tell them to fuck off. I mean, if your mates started to say hello by punching you in the face, you'd do something about it, right? So why not just say to them, "Look, I don't like having my head in your armpit while you whack me on the back like Hulk Hogan, can't we just shake hands, or wave at each other or something?"

Dear Dr. Ozzy:

I've suddenly developed a habit of putting my foot in my mouth in the most cringeworthy ways imaginable—like blurting out jokes about fat people in front of overweight friends. What could be causing this sudden outbreak of tactlessness? It's not booze, because it's happened as many times sober as it has when I'm drunk.

Fred, Basingstoke

It won't make you feel any better, but we all drop a clanger every now and again. You can't beat yourself up about it too much, 'cos life would be pretty boring if we all talked like politicians. And believe me, your fat joke's nothing compared with the shit I used to say when I was drinking four bottles of cognac a day. One time, I had to call up Brian Wilson from the Beach Boys after a big night out and say I was sorry for telling him I was glad his brother had just died. That was about 20 years ago, and I'm still cringing now.

Dear Dr. Ozzy:

I'm a happily married man, but I keep getting inappropriate e-mails from a male co-worker. Some are just dirty jokes, but others are graphic fantasies, like how he wants to sodomize me in the handicapped bathroom stall. At first it was funny, but now it's creepy and I want it to stop. Obviously I don't want to say anything to the boss.
"Marcus," California

If someone I knew started sending me e-mails about sticking their one-eyed wonder anywhere near my rear end— joke or otherwise—I wouldn't be writing to Dr. Ozzy for advice, I'd be using my mouth to tell him to stop giving me the fucking creeps, man. I mean, how about sending this sicko a reply that says, *"Don't ever e-mail me again"*? If that doesn't work, confront him in private. Failing that, get yourself a sexual harassment lawyer.

Dear Dr. Ozzy,

I recently took in a lodger, who said he was only going to be staying only a fortnight—but he's still here, six months later. Worse than that: he coughs all the time. It's driving me crazy. What can I do to get rid of him, or the cough, or both? Thank you.
Maddy, Cambridge

I've never had an annoying lodger, but I did once have a next-door neighbour who played tennis at midnight. It doesn't sound like much, but believe me, you don't want to hear *thwock, thwack, thwock* when you're trying to get some shut-eye. It was like living on centre court at Wimbledon. In the end, I set up my billion-watt PA system in the garden, and the second I heard him starting to play, I blasted some thrash metal in his direction. That soon put a stop to it. The same thing would solve your lodger problem, I reckon. After a few sessions of "The Best of Goatwhore"—highly recommended, by the way—he'll be begging to leave. And it'll drown out his coughing in the meantime.

Dear Dr. Ozzy,
I work at a bank and my boss urinates with the door open. It makes me very uncomfortable. What can I do?
Anonymous
Bakersfield, California

To be fair to your boss, when men get the call of nature, it's a very powerful urge. Our brains aren't set up to think about all the other stuff involved, like doors, seat lids . . or if the wall we're about to use is part of an important historic monument like the Alamo (I had no idea). Personally, I'm impressed the guy's even making it to the bathroom. If I was stuck in a bank all day, I'd get so fucking bored, I'd be pissing out of the window, trying to hit people standing at the cash machine outside. So I really think you should give the guy a break. Better yet, next time he empties his bladder in full view of his staff, get your colleagues to give him a round of applause and a score out of ten.

Dear Dr. Ozzy:
My best friend is being bullied, and he's now very depressed—he hasn't been at school for the past two weeks. I wish I could help, but we're in different grades (if don't see the bullying taking place, I can't tell a teacher). What should I do?
David, Boston

Tell his parents. You *must* tell his parents. Bullying is a terrible thing, and has fucked up a lot of people's lives. It's all very well to say people should just put up with it—or that it makes you stronger—if it ain't *your* head being flushed down the toilet on a daily basis. My bet is that if you tell this kid's folks, they'll be round the school in no time to sort it out. Do it now before it goes too far and something tragic happens, or you'll never forgive yourself.

Dear Dr. Ozzy:

My friends tell me I'm incredibly tight-fisted. Personally, I don't think this is fair: I just like to keep track of my spending and try to avoid throwing my heard-earned cash away. Should I listen to them? Should these people even really be my friends?

Jaycee, Surrey

There's a world of difference between "careful" and "tight as a duck's arse." I remember when I used to own a wine bar and restaurant—"Osbourne's" in Newport, Shropshire—there was a bloke who was so cheap, he'd come in and count his fucking peas. Literally. He'd tap me on the shoulder and go, "How come I got seven peas and my wife got twelve?" Then there's the kind of tightwad who claims to be on a diet when it comes to ordering food, but then scavenges from everyone else's plates. The "See Food" diet, as I always call it. But anyway, back to your question: the fact is, if your friends are saying they're offended by your behaviour, chances are you're tighter than Elvis Presley's spandex. So it can't hurt to dig deep for a while, just to prove 'em wrong.

Dear Dr. Ozzy:

Help! I just sent a long and emotional e-mail about how much I hate my job to my best friend in Sweden, only I accidentally (don't ask how) copied my boss. What should I do?

Margaret, New York

Start looking for a new job.

Dear Dr. Ozzy:

I know you're supposed to make eye contact when talking to new people, but how far do you take it—the occasional glance (if so, how many seconds?) or a continuous full-lock?

Ken, Woking

It ain't a full-lock and it ain't a glance—it's something in-between. But it's very important to get it right, 'cos it's not comfortable being around people who can't look you in the eye when they're having a conversation. They seem dodgy. Whatever you do, though, don't *stare*—if your eyes are bugging out like you're some kind of nutter, that ain't cool. To me, it's all about giving off a warm vibe; making others feel at ease. Maybe if you stop counting how many seconds there are between every blink, it'll come naturally.

Dear Dr. Ozzy:
My colleague (the next cubicle over) has terrible body odour. How can I break the news to him gently—or is there a way of dealing with the smell without having to confront him?
Marie, Stoke on Trent

Fuck I take a shower ever day, so it pisses me off when other people don't give their friends and colleagues the same courtesy. Unfortunately, though, there's no painless answer to your problem. You could move cubicles, I suppose. Or put an anonymous gift of deodorant on his desk. But the best solution is to confront him—in a nice way. Say, "Next time you're in the bath, why don't you try turning on the taps?"

Dear Dr. Ozzy,
Excuse my French, but my boss is an arsehole. His idea of management is to boast about every pathetic little thing he does while belittling everyone else's achievements. How can I get him to change his ways?
Sarah, Stoke

Why not get together with your colleagues who feel the same way and have an intervention? Or, if it's a bigger company, complain to human resources (or whatever they call it). Failing that, leave. That's what I used to do when I hated a job. Either that, or I behaved so badly—like stealing cows' eyeballs from the slaughterhouse where I worked and putting them in girls' drinks at the pub across the road—they kicked me out. Jobs are harder to find these days, of course, so that might not be a good idea. Unfortunately, that also makes idiots like your boss think they're God.

Try not to give him the pleasure.

Dear Dr. Ozzy:

A friend of mine visited my house the other day when I was recovering from a case of winter sniffles. When he came down with his own cold a few days after, he sent me an angry e-mail telling me that I should have warned him I had germs. Is this fair?
Neil, Stevenage

No. How does this guy know where he got the cold from, anyway? And even if you *did* give it to him, what's everyone supposed to do, walk around in germ-sealed plastic bags wearing face masks and rubber gloves all the time? Give me a break.

Dear Ozzy:

I play football after work with my colleagues, and last week my boss broke my ankle with a dirty tackle. I'm furious with him, and want revenge—but I don't want to get fired. Any ideas?
Guglielmo, Rome

Two words, Guglielmo: shit happens. If you're gonna kick a ball around, you've got to accept that some people's personalities change beyond recognition when scoring goals is involved. I learned that lesson years ago, when I played on my local pub team every Sunday morning. Well, I say "played," but it was really just an excuse to air my brain out after the night before. I soon realised that the blokes who were perfectly normal and friendly while having a few beers turned into wild fucking animals on the field. I mean, they just forgot who they were, to the point where they lost all self-respect... then five minutes later they were back down the pub, as nice as you like again. So you should forget about revenge, 'cos you can't live your life trying get back at people for things you should have seen coming in the first place. Stop playing if it really bothers you. Otherwise get back on the field and try to run a bit faster next time.

Dear Dr. Ozzy:

My neighbour plays his Elton John record collection at full-blast every Sunday morning—the one day of the week when I get to sleep in. No offense to Sir Elton (I know he's a friend of yours) but what can I do to banish "Rocket Man" from my life for good?
Adriana, Bergamo, Italy

Ask him nicely to turn it down, and if that doesn't work, buy some earplugs—unless you want to start a feud. Also, let's face it: the situation could be worse. He could be playing Justin Bieber.

DR. OZZY'S INCREDIBLY HELPFUL TIPS—

Your Boss Is an Arsehole If...

- He makes himself Employee of the Month. Every month.
- He docks your salary for the day you take off to go to your mum's funeral.
- He uses the stopwatch on his iPhone to time your toilet breaks.
- He thinks the stopwatch on his iPhone is a "pretty cool app." But not as cool as "Pull My Finger"—which he plays with in his office while everyone else is working their butts off.
- He gets you wasted after work, then shaves off your eyebrows when you pass out. Oh, hang on a minute... that was *me*...

- He gives you a choice between working at the weekend or giving him a blowjob.
- He promotes people based on how many times they *don't* work at the weekend.
- At a team-bonding event, he thinks it's hilarious to shoot a paintball at your lovesack.

Dear Dr. Ozzy:
How do you cope with people who plot against you, but are as nice as pie to your face?
David, Woking

Number one: don't ever work in TV, 'cos the industry is crawling with back-stabber types. Number two: you don't have to "cope" with them—just avoid them like the plague. Unless you're wearing handcuffs or have been slammed in a prison cell, you don't *have* to be in anyone's company (although I know it can be difficult with co-workers and bosses). I mean, if someone has B.O., you don't choose to sit next to them, do you? It's same with people who have toxic personalities. If it's an option, get up and walk away.

Dear Dr. Ozzy:
Is it just me, or is it basically impossible for men to make new friends when they're married with kids, given that the pub is now out of bounds (at least on a regular basis)?
Chaz, Isle of Wight

That's why God invented golf and fishing. Both of these things let men get out of the house and socialise with each other without getting a stage-five bollocking the next day. The trouble is, if you don't have the patience for that stuff—I certainly don't—there ain't many other options. And it's not as if someone like *me* can go out for the occasional quiet pint, either. One whiff of the old devil's brew, and the next thing you know it's 4 a.m., I'm blasted to kingdom come, and trying to drive my car through the front door. So for me the last refuge has always been the toilet. You might not make any new friends in there, but when the kids are rioting and the wife's on your case, I highly recommend it as a way of taking a quick break.

Dear Dr. Ozzy:
Is it worth staying in touch with old friends—from high school, etc.—when you no longer have anything in common. Or is it better and more honest to just make a clean break?
Julian, Newport

Move on. The fact is, you're a different person now than when you were a kid, so unless your old classmates have gone into the same kind of job or whatever, it's pointless going through the awkwardness of meeting up for a beer once every ten years. Having said that, it's sometimes interesting to see what became of the dickheads at school. I remember this one guy: he always wore the uniform (even though you didn't have to), always did his homework on time, always came top of everything. Meanwhile, I was the prankster, thief, and school goldfish murderer. He ended up being a bus inspector. I became a rock star. Sometimes I have a good old chuckle about that.

Dear Dr. Ozzy:
As a boss, I'm struggling to deal with a worker who's not a "team player." Short of firing him, which seems a bit excessive, what's the best way to manage such a difficult personality? I'm sure you have plenty of experience as the leader of a rock band.
David, Surrey

I have a rule in my band: if there's something you don't like about your job, or if you've been offered a better gig somewhere else, all I ask is for a bit of notice before you leave. And it's the same in reverse. So if I were you, I'd have a chat with this guy, tell him it ain't working out, and suggest he finds a new job by the end of the year. On the other hand, if he's doing excellent work and the only problem is that you don't like him, I'd suggest you just deal with it, 'cos talented people are hard to find, and your employees don't have to be your friends. If no-one else at your company likes him, either, then that's a different matter, 'cos he'll be affecting morale. In that case he has to go.

Dr. Ozzy's Trivia Quiz: Personal Skills

Find the answers—and tote up your score—on page 263

1. How do you say hello to close friend in Northern Mozambique?
   a) Kiss them on the nose
   b) Shake your fist at head level and shout, "*Wooshay! Wooshay!*"
   c) Clap three times

2. According to the etiquette people at Debrett's, what shouldn't you "glance longingly" at during dinner?
   a) The best-looking person at the table
   b) Your wife's tits
   c) Your iPhone

3. How many friends does the average person have on Facebook?
   a) 130
   b) 95
   c) 260

4. What did a New Zealand bank manager do in 2006 that made him Worst Boss of the Year?
   a) Ordered female tellers to show at least three inches of cleavage
   b) Had his staff tied up and robbed
   c) Banned toilet breaks during office hours

5. When the workers at a Lithuanian-owned car dealership in Atlanta, USA, asked for a raise, what did the boss do?
   a) Shoot them
   b) Kill himself
   c) Sue them for emotional distress

The Jelly Between
Your Ears

9

It Ain't Easy, Being Mental

Most of us spend more time washing the dishes than we do taking care of our mental health. It's unbelievable, when you think about it, 'cos of all the things that can go wrong with us, "not feeling yourself" is right up there with the worst. It ain't exactly rare, either. According to real doctors*, one in four people come down with some kind of major freak-out at some point in their lives. The trouble is, even today, people don't like to talk about it. I mean, when you go to work in the morning and the boss says, "How are you?" no-one wants to go, "Oh, I'm feeling a bit *mentally ill* today, actually." You'd end up in a padded room, wearing pyjamas with no fucking sleeves.

Luckily, you can always come to Dr. Ozzy for advice. I've been through just about everything you can imagine: depression, panic attacks, drug abuse, cries for help, alcohol abuse, obsessive compulsive disorder... you name it, man. And the

---

* At the World Health Organisation.

one thing I've learned: no matter how much you don't want to, you've *gotta* talk about it. Go to your GP. See a therapist. Confide in friends (although it's usually better to find someone who ain't biased). If you keep your problems bottled up instead, they'll only get worse over time. Having said all that, if you grew up in England when I did, the whole idea of talking about anything is a fucking joke. If someone had any kind of anxiety or depression when I was a kid, it was called a "nervous breakdown"—and people only ever mentioned it in hushed voices, behind closed doors. But times have changed. Treatments have improved. And people are beginning to realise that *everyone* has issues, and everyone needs to get them out in the open if they want to move on. So that's what this chapter is about: coming clean, clearing the air, and hopefully taking the first step towards getting *real* help from someone who ain't me.

Dear Dr. Ozzy:
My friends have started to tell me that I'm way too paranoid—
about my boss, my girlfriend, the government...you name it. Isn't
a bit of paranoia good for you, though?
Jamie, New York

No. Being paranoid's a terrible way to live. For example: every so often when I get on a plane, I convince myself that it's doomed, and that everyone's gonna die. So I spend the whole twelve hours in the air sweating and trying to stop my heart jumping out of my ribcage...which is a total waste of time, 'cos my panic attack ain't exactly gonna stop a bomb going off, or the autopilot breaking down. I mean, I suppose you could argue that being a worrier makes you more likely to live longer, but if you're feeling paranoid 24/7, what kind of life are you living anyway? It ain't comfortable for the people around you, either—especially not if you're giving your girlfriend the Gestapo treatment every time she comes home. Listen to your mates and chill out, man.

Dear Dr. Ozzy:
Can you finally explain why is it so bloody hard for men to cry?
Abigail, Wexham

It's not that it's hard, it's just that we don't particularly enjoy it. I mean, yeah, every now and again—like once a decade—a good old cry clears the air. But it ain't something your average bloke wants to do on a regular basis, 'cos it's exhausting. Women, on the other hand, can't seem to get enough of it. For example: my wife insists on going to see these awful films— "slurpies," I call 'em—where you spend the whole time feeling like your gran's just died. I can still remember the last one I was dragged to: *The Notebook*. By the time the credits rolled, I was just about having a nervous breakdown—then I thought to myself, "Why am I sitting here, in darkened room, feeling all unnecessarily choked up?" When I looked over at Sharon, she was even more puffy-faced and snotty than I was. Then she goes, "Oooh, wasn't that brilliant, Ozzy?" At moments like that, I think that men and women might as well be from different universes.

Hi Dr. Ozzy:
I suffer from a condition known as bipolar, which makes me impulsive and harm people when I don't mean to. It started when my father began drinking a case of beer every night. He would get rowdy and mean and drive me to school when he was drunk. Now he's divorcing my sweet mom. Could this be the cause of my problems?
Christina, Texas

I strongly suggest you find a good therapist. And by that I mean someone who has in-depth knowledge of bipolar— not your local GP, who'll probably tell you to take an aspirin and sleep it off. I'm not bipolar myself, but I've been to the dark side more than a few occasions, and therapy has helped me a great deal over the years. It basically gives you a different view of the things you think might have caused your problems—like your old man's drinking—'cos when you're in the depths of a mental freak-out, you often don't understand why, and you end up blaming it on the stuff and the people around you. In other words, you end up telling yourself that the way you *see* the world is the way it is... when in reality your problems could have been caused by one of many, many things. You might also need anti-depressants, or some other kind of drug, but—as strange as this might sound coming from an addict like me—I honestly believe that in your case, therapy is the best medication. Or at least it's a good first step.

DR. OZZY'S INSANE-BUT-TRUE STORIES

History's Biggest Nutters

◆ **Joan of Arc:** Cross-dressing French teenager who led armies into battle and got burned at the stake—at an age when the worst thing most chicks have to deal with is Bieber Fever. Some think her "visions from God" were caused by bovine tuberculosis, from unpasteurized milk.

◆ **Pythagoras:** Brainy Greek. Loved animals and triangles. Also fucking crazy. For example: the guy was totally freaked out by beans. Good job he never had to sit in a confined area with me after a burrito.

◆ **Charles the Mad:** French king who thought he was made of glass (he had his pants reinformed with iron bars in case he fell over and shattered). The guy was so nuts, he couldn't even remember his own name. I feel sorry for the poor fucker who had to keeping reminding him: "Your Royal Highness's name is *Charles the Mad*, Sir."

◆ **Wolfgang Amadeus Mozart:** Totally mental German composer. Suffered from attention deficit disorder, bipolar disorder, and Tourette's syndrome. The real title of *Piano Concerto No. 24 in C-Minor* is actually *Piano Concerto No. 24 in C-Fucking Minor, You Asshole.*

◆ **Lord Byron:** English poet. Mad as a bag of pissed-off ferrets. Had a pet bear at college—and a litterbox the size of Buckingham Palace. Later, when he got bored of writing soppy verses, he formed his own navy and declared war on the Turks. (This is true, honestly.) Then he caught a cold and died.

Dear Dr. Ozzy:

I can't control my temper. I finally realised this when I recently spent the night in jail after punching someone in the face for "looking at me funny." What can I do to calm myself down?

Graham, Yorkshire

Generally speaking, people don't just wake up angry. There's got to be an underlying cause—something in your past, or maybe even just anxiety. Anger is a *symptom*. Beer also fuels anger: once, a long time ago, I hit someone with a bottle in a pub when I was blasted out of my mind, and it still haunts me to this day. So if you drink, you'd better think about stopping immediately. If I were you, I'd also get some anger management therapy. If you think that sounds like a joke from an Adam Sandler movie, wait and see how funny it is when you hit someone again and get 20 years for grievous bodily harm.

Dear Dr. Ozzy:

A few months ago I was laid-off from the company I'd been with for ten years, and although I've found another job since—with better

opportunities—I can't stop dwelling on how I was let go, and it's
making me grumpy and depressed. Should I see a shrink?
Mark, Cleethorpes

I know exactly how you feel, Mark. I was fired by my
old band, Black Sabbath, in 1979. I mean, granted, I was a
horrendous alcoholic—but it wasn't like they were all fucking
choirboys, either. Just to make things worse, it was my best
friend Bill Ward who broke the news to me. I can't remember
the specifics, 'cos I was shitfaced on beer and cognac on the
day it happened, but I'll never forget how bad it felt. After
ten years, you're practically married to what you do for a
living. When you're given the boot, it's like going through a
divorce—even if you know in your heart it's the right thing.
It might be that you're just angry, in which case I would
definitely recommend going to see a shrink. Otherwise,
getting over it will just take time. Whatever you do, don't try
and vent your frustrations in other ways. In my case, I set fire
to my back garden, shot all my chickens, and went to the pub,
but it only made me feel worse.

I still feel bad for the poor chickens to this day.

Dear Dr. Ozzy:
I have a terrible, gnawing sense of dread about the state of the
world—in particular the environment. (According to the news, this
has been the wettest\driest\hottest\coldest winter on record for just
about any country you care to mention.) Is this anxiety normal? Is
there anything any of us can really do about it?
Carel, Dubai

Number one: stop watching the TV or browsing the
internet. Number two: replace the time you've been spending
doing those thing with something healthier and more
constructive. Me, I like to draw. Just doodles, really. But it's
a great release. Don't get me wrong, I ain't saying we should
all just bury our heads in the sand. But the point of the news

is to keep you watching the news—so they only focus on the most horrendous stuff. If you're sensitive to it, you can literally make yourself sick. In fact, I once heard about a guy who had inoperable cancer, and he went to a Chinese doctor, who told him, "Here's what I want you to do: get rid of your TV, get rid of your radio, switch off your computer. Just focus on the positive." After three months, he was in remission. I ain't saying he was cured by giving up *News at Ten*. But I bet it made him a lot happier.

Dear Dr. Ozzy:
My GP recently put me on anti-depressants. Are there any side-effects I should know about?
David, Surrey

Anti-depressants are fabulous things, David, but they'll play havoc with your meat and two veg. I've been taking them for years and what I've found is, I can get a boner, but no fireworks. So I just end up pumping away on top of Sharon like a road drill all night. I tried Viagra once, but by the time it kicked in, the missus was fast asleep. So it was just me and this tent pole in front of me, with nothing to do but watch the History Channel.

DR. OZZY'S AMAZING MEDICAL MISCELLANY

Crazy, Even for Mental Disorders

- **Capgras Syndrome.** When you're convinced that everyone around you has been replaced with an identical imposter. If you happen to be a Third World dictator who's hired a lot of body-doubles, this might be true. For everyone else, it's a sign you need to catch the next bus to the funny farm.

- **Paris Syndrome.** This one affects only Japanese people. It happens when they go to Paris expecting paradise, meet the French—especially rude waiters—and can't handle it, to the point where they have a total meltdown. I ain't taking the piss. The Japanese embassy now has a 24-hour helpline for tourists who come down with it. There are usually about twenty cases a year.*
- **Walking-Corpse Syndrome.** Sufferers think they're dead, and that life is a dream they're having while in heaven (or hell). I thought I had this once, but luckily it turned out I wasn't delusional—I was actually dead. It was only temporary while I was in a coma (after my quad bike crash).

Dear Dr. Ozzy:
I keep waking up in the night after hearing loud noises, but my wife (asleep beside me) hears nothing. Could this be the so-called "Exploding Head Syndrome" that I heard about on television, or do you think it's just a common-or-garden nightmare?
Ted, Bath

Unless you've got a pet hamster who's throwing bricks out of his cage in the middle of the night, it seems unlikely that there'd be enough loud noises to make you wake up on such a regular basis. On the other hand, it's plausible that your wife could be sleeping through whatever it is that's disturbing you. My own wife sleeps like she's been dead twenty-five years. A Boeing 747 full of atomic bombs could crash into our back garden, and she'd be none the wiser the next morning. By the sound of it, though, this is probably all in your own mind. As

---
*www.parissyndrome.info

for "exploding head syndrome"...I've had a few hangovers that might fit that description, but in your case it's more likely to be a bad case of anxiety dreams. Try some relaxation techniques before bed, and let me know how it goes.

Dear Dr. Ozzy,
After all the tragic shootings in America, I'm curious if you think it's possible to tell in advance that a mentally ill person is going to "snap," or if it's out of anyone's control?
Jake, Los Angeles

To me, it's not a question of being able to tell when someone's gonna snap, it's the fact that it's ridiculously easy for a crazy person to get hold of a gun in America. I mean, I should know: I'm a complete nutjob, and I own several guns. All I had to do was show the guy in the shop my ID and wait a few weeks. In England, on the other hand, a copper had to come over to my house and interview me before they'd let me keep a firearm. I've got nothing against guns in general, but if the government makes people take a test before they can drive a car, why not have the same kind of rule for when you buy a Glock? They say it ain't guns that kill people, it's people who kill people...but it seems to me like it would be a lot fucking harder for a lunatic to become a mass-murderer if he had to use an old frying pan instead of a semi-automatic.

Dear Dr. Ozzy:
My 19-year-old son has started to suffer from panic attacks, usually during exams, job interviews, that kind of thing. Next week he has his driving test (third attempt) and I'm wondering, is there's anything safe I can give him to calm him down?
Janet, Surrey

If it makes you feel any better, it took me 19 attempts to pass my driving test—and I only finally became legal in October 2009. Not that it ever stopped me driving, mind you: if anyone ever asked me if I had a licence, I'd just say, "Oh yes"...which was sort of true: I had a TV licence. About the nerves, though: I know exactly how your son feels. I used to get so intimidated by the examiner, I'd have a few of pints before getting in the car. But then I'd forget basic things, like which side of road to drive on. Eventually I went to my GP and asked him for some pills to chill me out, so he wrote me a prescription for a sedative. The box said, "WARNING: DO NOT MIX WITH ALCOHOL"—so to be safe, I smoked half a brick of Afghan hash instead. The good news: when I got into the car, I didn't feel intimidated at all. The bad news: when I stopped for a red light, I nodded off. So to answer your question: yes, there are (legal) drugs your son can take—ask your GP. But nerves are better than being too relaxed for your own good.

Dear Dr. Ozzy:
You often talk about "vibes" and "energy," so it's clear that you feel things that other people don't . . . do you think people can develop intuition, or are they just born that way?
Sharon, Massachusetts

Most of the time it's just common sense. I remember when Princess Diana was still alive, for example. I woke up one morning and said to Tony, my personal assistant, "You know what, something bad's gonna happen to her." And sure enough, a few days or weeks later, she was dead. It was terribly sad. Tony said me to later, "Whatever you do, Ozzy, don't have any premonitions about *me*." But the fact is, if someone's living their life at 300mph, you don't have to be a clairvoyant to see what's coming. I think some people have better intuition than others, but there ain't anything magical about it.

Dear Dr. Ozzy:
I recently had to speak in public, and I became so nervous my vision became blurred. Is this "hysterical blindness"?
Nicola, Cheshire

Panic attacks can do all kinds of weird things to you—I know, 'cos I've suffered from stage fright all my life. I went to see my GP about it once and he told me, "Trying getting a brown paper bag and blowing into it." I said to him, "Apart from filling a bag with air, what the fuck is that gonna do?" He didn't take too kindly to that. I see a therapist now to treat my anxiety—it's been doing me a lot of good—although anything to do with your sight is so important, it might also be worth seeing an eye doctor. The problem is that your symptoms probably only appear when you're nervous. So you might have to invite an audience and recite some Shakespeare while he checks you out.

Dear Dr. Ozzy,
Every time I leave the house, I have to go back two or three times to re-check that the door is locked, or that the oven isn't on, or that the burglar alarm is set. What's wrong with me?
Karen, Surrey

A lot of people would tell you that you're "a bit OCD"—in other words, that you've got obsessive compulsive disorder. To be honest with you, though, I think that might be over-egging it. Everyone seems to have OCD these days. But worrying about leaving the door open is *normal*, especially if you have bad short-term memory, like I do. I mean, no-one wants to come home and find a homeless bloke with his trousers down, taking a shit on the coffee table. But the reality is, even if you did leave the door open, nothing bad would probably happen. You're over-thinking things. It happened to me the other night: I was home alone, and I spent the entire time crapping myself over every little rustle and creak. Then when Sharon came back early without any warning, I just about dived under the bed for my sniper rifle. It's a good job I was too groggy to go any faster—shooting the missus would have earned me a right old bollocking.

DR. OZZY'S AMAZING MEDICAL MISCELLANY

Old-Fashioned Treatments...to Avoid

+ **Insulin-Coma.** Back in the day, some bright spark thought that if they shot you up with enough insulin to put you into a coma, you'd wake up cured from drug addiction and/or schizophrenia. It worked brilliantly— apart from one small problem: the "waking up" bit. A lot of people didn't.

+ **Trepanation.** If you complained about "personal demons" in the Middle Ages, they'd strap you to a table while some fat, dribbling peasant wearing a potato sack went at your skull with a hammer and chisel. The idea was to make a big enough hole to "let the demons out." Unfortunately, more often than not, half your brains came out with 'em.

+ **Hydrotherapy.** It wasn't a good idea to suffer from hyperactivity disorder, or *any* kind of disorder, in Victorian times. You'd end up locked up in the loony bin, chained to a wall, and blasted in the face with a fireman's hose—until you "calmed down." A lot of times you calmed down so much you didn't have a pulse any more.

Dear Dr. Ozzy,
I've just found out that a friend of mind is undergoing a course of
electro-shock treatment for depression. It sounds terrible to me, and
I want her to stop. What do you think?
Mary, Dorset

When you hear the phrase "electro-shock treatment" you immediately think of *One Flew Over the Cuckoo's Nest.* But a very close friend of mine had this done, and apparently it's nothing like it was in 1930s, when they used to basically plug you into the mains and see what happened. For a start, it's called "electroconvulsive therapy" now. The only thing I would suggest is asking your friend if she's absolutely sure that she's tried everything else, because from what I understand, it's one of those if-all-else-fails things. My friend swears that it cured her, but I've gotta say, I'm not sure I'd ever be miserable enough to hook myself up to one of those machines.

Dear Dr. Ozzy:
Having a strict routine makes me happy—I have an OCD-type
personality and anxiety—but I worry that it's also turning me into
the world's most boring person. What should I do?
Amelia, Boston, U.S.A.

Sometimes you've gotta make yourself unhappy to be happy. I mean, if you think about it, there's an up and down to almost everything worth doing—and the down usually comes first. For example: I get horrendously anxious before gigs, but I love the adrenaline rush I get on stage. Maybe you need to test yourself a bit; do things that you make you feel nervous, and see if you like the sense of achievement you get later on. If you don't, and you're happier in bed at 9 p.m. every night with a cup of tea and a crossword, then stick to your routine. Better happy and boring than interesting and miserable.

Dear Dr. Ozzy:

A close friend of mine has become very angry with God, blaming Him for all his recent career, health, and romantic disappointments (of which there have been many). Now I've read on the Internet that this is a actually a kind of mental disorder. Should I be worried?

Fredo, London

Most of us are taught from birth to believe in a God with a beard who lives on a fluffy white cloud or whatever, so if someone's having a terrible run of luck, it's ain't exactly surprising that they might end up blaming Him. Instead of worrying about your friend going mad—it certainly doesn't sound like a "mental disorder" to me—why not talk to him; give him a shoulder to cry on. He needs your support, not your internet research.

Dr. Ozzy's Trivia Quiz: Grey Matter

Find the answers—and tote up your score—on page 263

1. Which of these are real mental disorders?
   a) Bigorexia
   b) Foreign Accent Syndrome
   c) Jumping Frenchman Disorder

2. If you were a hybristophiliac, what might you want to do?
   a) Marry a mass murderer
   b) Have two different personalities
   c) Have sex with your Toyota Prius

3. This statement about the human brain is true:
   a) There aren't any "pain receptors" in your brain, so if Hannibal Lecter started to eat it, you wouldn't feel a thing
   b) While awake, your brain generates enough power to light a 100 w bulb
   c) Music is the biggest trigger of emotional memories

4. How many thoughts does the average person have every day (roughly)?
   a) 600
   b) 70,000
   c) 1 million

5. How many prescriptions for anti-depressant drugs are handed out every year in America (estimated)?
   a) 18 million
   b) 81 million
   c) 118 million

Sex, Romance & Ballcare

10

Dr. Ozzy's Guide to the Bats
and the Bees

If you've come to the Prince of Darkness for sex advice, you're already in big fucking trouble. It ain't that I don't have a lot of experience in the bedroom department—I've got my fair share of war stories, like any other rocker—it's just that I wasn't conscious for most of it. Back in the 1970s, most chicks used to light up a cigarette after a good old bonk. Not the ones I slept with: they were too busy calling for an ambulance.

Still, I've picked up a few pearls of wisdom here and there, which is a good job, 'cos at least half the questions I get, especially at *Rolling Stone*, are from people with sex problems—or romance problems, or ball problems. Or, more often than you'd think, a combination of all three. To make things easy, I've rolled them all into this chapter. Just remember: there's more to life than mind-blowing sex. And if you find out what it is, let me know.

I: SEX

Dear Dr. Ozzy:

When my girlfriend takes Ambien, she turns into an insatiable sexual freak. In the morning, though, she has no memory of it. Is it wrong for me to go along with this?

Rob, California

It sounds like I need to send my Ambien back to the pharmacy and ask for a refund: when Sharon takes it, she turns into an insatiable fucking snorer, not a sexual freak. Having said that, if your girlfriend doesn't remember any of these epic rogerings in the morning, it seems to me like it's dangerously close to date-rape. Aside from the fact that it ain't right, if she ever found out about it, and you had an argument and broke up or whatever, you could end up in leg-irons and a jumpsuit. I think a confession is in order.

Dear Dr. Ozzy:

I gave my wife a vibrator as a gift. Now, every night when she thinks I'm asleep, I can hear her using next to me. We're barely having sex, and I'm worried I can't compete with the machine. Please help.

Anonymous

Hide the batteries.

Dear Dr. Ozzy:

I've been sleeping on and off with an average-looking girl at work for a few months—usually after a Friday night session in the pub. Yesterday I found out she's updated her "relationship status" on Facebook and is calling me her boyfriend! I never wanted this to become serious. How can I tell her this without causing drama?

Jeff, Preston

First of all, you've got a lot of balls calling this girl "average-looking." What are *you*, Mr. fucking Brad Pitt? Secondly, if you go to bed with a girl more than once, you either have to explain to her that it ain't serious—and run the risk of her not shagging you any more—or be a man and stop doing it, 'cos she's gonna get hurt. You also need to ask yourself the question: "How would I feel if this were the other way around?" I mean, men are very good at saying, "Oh, it's nothing, just the occasional shag," but then if another bloke comes on the scene, they're like wild animals marking their territory. Make up your mind how you feel, then stop messing this poor girl around.

Dear Dr. Ozzy,
I have a policy of not advising people on their love lives. However, I suspect my friend "Bob" (not his real name) might be having an extra-marital relationship with a neighbour, largely because he likes her breasts. If this was your mate, would you offer advice?
John, Aberdeen

No. Trust me—stay away. It's impossible to know all the facts in these situations, and you probably wouldn't want to. Meanwhile, if he ever asks you to start covering for him, just say, "What you do is none of my business, don't ever ask about this again, I don't want to know." Otherwise you're putting your head in the lion's den, and sooner or later, two slobbering jaws are gonna come chomping down on your neck, I guarantee it. The only time you'd have any reason to pipe up would be if someone was getting hurt, or if the situation became horrendous—like he started bringing his bit-on-the-side over to your house for dinner. In that case, it would be worth a quiet word.

Dear Dr. Ozzy,
Why do men always want young girlfriends? Young people are boring: they don't have good stories to tell or interesting views to share. Do men think only with their trousers?
Darla, Helsinki, Finland

The truth is, men have *two* brains: the one in their heads and the one in their Y-fronts. The one nearer the floor usually wins—that's why you see these guys walking around in Los Angeles with bald spots and pony tails. In fact, a friend of mine who's 63 came over to my house the other day in his sports car with some young female in the passenger seat who might as well have been his great-granddaughter. I said to him, "Where do you find these girls? *Pre-school?*" He just laughed. But I guarantee it won't make him happy for long, 'cos one day they'll be lying in bed and he'll want to talk about Colonel Gaddafi, and she'll think he's talking about the guy who invented fried chicken. (In response to this question, a guy called "Peter" from West Sussex wrote to me, saying: "Ask Darla from Helsinki why men should NOT have young girlfriends? I sail, ski, work-out three days a week, and prefer slim and energetic companions as opposed to my overweight, TV-watching contemporaries. PS: I am 81 years old.")

Dear Dr. Ozzy:
How do you make a girl reach orgasm?
Andre, St. Albans, Hertfordshire

I've always been too busy giving *myself* an orgasm to pay much attention. If you find out, let me know.

Dear Dr. Ozzy:
I'm a 28-year-old woman who has never—not once!—reached orgasm. I enjoy sex but it's more like a good aerobic workout than something mind-blowing. Am I choosing the wrong guys, or do I have some kind of deep psychological handicap? Please help.
Sanna, Helsinki, Finland

Dr. Ozzy is a bit out of his depth on this one (see above), but the first thing to do is look at the side-effects of any pills you're taking. For example, anti-depressants wreak havoc in my own screaming ecstasy department—but I don't know what the deal is for women. Maybe also buy one of those electronic "back massager" wands, then practice trying to get yourself over-the-top on your own. The better you know your own body, the better chance you have of learning what sets you off. Failing that... give me a call.

Dear Dr. Ozzy:
After I have sex my feet tingle. What's happening? Bad circulation? Return of blood to my feet?
Daniel, New Hampshire

Let me ask you something: Are you one of those blokes who likes to wear ladies' underwear? Because I once knew a girl who wore tights during a game of hide-the-sausage, and her feet fell asleep halfway through. Maybe that's your problem. Either that, or get rid of the ropes and the ballgag, and don't do it hanging upside down next time.

Dear Dr. Ozzy:
My boyfriend and I have been together for a long time. To spice up our sex life, he's suggested a threesome with one of his college mates. Does this make him gay?
Anonymous

Call me a boring old turd, but I've always preferred sex when it's done on a one-at-a-time basis. With more than one dick swinging around the place, you might end up with a black eye, or—God forbid—getting one of 'em stuck in the wrong place. To answer your question, though, it sounds to me more like your boyfriend's bi, not gay. Then again, his buddy might be gay. You could spend the evening with nothing to do but watch two hairy blokes go at it hammer and tongs, which wouldn't be much fun. And what if you end up liking the other guy more than your boyfriend? Trust me, threesomes might look good on telly, but they're usually more trouble than they're worth.

Dear Dr. Ozzy:

My friend and I—both married men—have been reliving old times by going out drinking and chatting up women, but stopping before any actual infidelity takes place. We call them "dry runs," because they give us the thrill of the chase without breaking any rules.
Is this wrong?

Michael, London

Playing with matches is a lot of fun, Michael, but at some point your wig's gonna catch fire. There's just no way this can end well for you. One night you'll have too many drinks, you'll do a "dry run" on a woman whose beautiful and single, she'll make the first move, and before you know it, you'll be signing your divorce papers. You're creating temptation for yourself, which means trouble is only two steps behind. Get a lapdance if you're desperate for a quick thrill, or better yet, take the missus away for a dirty weekend.

DR. OZZY'S INSANE-BUT-TRUE STORIES

If You Think *Human* Sex Is Weird...

- When a male bee, or drone, gets lucky, his balls literally *fall off* inside the virgin queen. This stops her getting knocked up by anyone else. It also hurts.
- If you think human blokes have it bad, spare a thought for male giraffes. For starters, sex is limited to a two-week period every *year* (the only time females are up for it). And it ain't exactly much to look forward to, anyway: before any action takes places, the female has to make absolutely sure that her mate is "Mr Right." She does this by pissing on his face.
- Female hyenas don't just wear the trousers in their relationships—they even get boners. That's 'cos they

have a "pseudopenis," which is basically a *massive* clitoris. I bet they have hairy armpits, too.

♦ Male bedbugs have gotta be the biggest bastards out there in the sex department. Instead of courting the female, or even bothering to give her a cuddle and feel her up a bit, he just stabs her in the chest with his spiky dick. Biologists have a term for it: "traumatic insemination." It's just fucking lazy, if you ask me.

Dear Dr. Ozzy:
I have an annoying habit of popping the champagne cork before the party gets under way. I've tried slowing down, and/or mentally re-tiling the kitchen to take my mind off things during the process, but no luck, alas. Any advice gratefully received.
Jezz, Hertfordshire

Is this code for something? This is *Dr. Ozzy* you're writing to, not the Archbishop of fucking Canterbury, so for God's sake spit it out, man. If you mean what I think you mean, why not just get on with it quicker? It'll give you and the missus more time to do the garden.

Dear Dr. Ozzy:
I have just turned 68 and have the opposite problem to your premature "cork popper" the other week. It doesn't matter how racy my thoughts—say, Jennifer Aniston in a maid's outfit—I still end up pumping away when the missus is ready for a cigarette. What can I do?
Dave, Wales

They have a word for this: "Anorgasmia." There's also another term, and it's called "being 68 years old." Unfortunately, as blokes get on a bit, *everything* to do with sex becomes difficult. If it's any consolation, the most exciting thing that happens in my bedroom most nights is an episode of *Law & Order*. Having said that, you should get your prostate checked out, and also ask your doctor about the side-effects of any drugs you're taking. Of course, you could also just be bored. Try thinking about Courteney Cox instead.

Dear Dr. Ozzy:

I have an embarrassing fetish (it's surprisingly common). I want my girlfriend to put me in a diaper and treat me like a big baby. My girlfriend and I are compatible in every way, but I'm terrified to ask her about this. What would you do?

Anonymous, USA

This one's a bit far-out even for Dr. Ozzy. I mean, there's plenty of time later in life to wear adult nappies, so why speed it up? Having said that, I had the opposite problem to you in my drinking days: Sharon was always *telling* me to wear nappies, 'cos I used to piss in the bed so often. I also used to shit my pants on a fairly regular basis, which ain't very fucking nice. I suppose if you start doing the same thing, your girlfriend might make the same suggestion, saving you the whole "I want to be a big baby" conversation.

Dear Dr. Ozzy:

I'm 29 years old and have become increasingly dependant on seriously hardcore porn to get turned on. Is this going to ruin my performance with real women?

Anonymous, USA

No. Women didn't stop getting knocked up when the internet was invented—although maybe their husbands don't pester them for sex as much, 'cos now they've got online filth on demand, 24 hours a day. The trouble is, even the XXX stuff gets boring very quickly: it's not like there's ever a surprise fucking ending. The trick is to ration your exposure, not try and find stronger and stronger stuff. If it ever gets to the point where there's crapping or donkeys involved, trust me, you've gone too far. Otherwise stop worrying.

Dear Dr. Ozzy:
I've just returned from a bachelor party in Las Vegas. Being married with kids, however, I'm concerned that the stripper with whom I, er, "relaxed" in a private booth might have given me oral herpes—we didn't do anything improper, although she did feed me strawberries and cream, mouth to mouth. Any words of wisdom?
Brian, Warrington

Forget oral herpes, Brian, it sounds to me like you've come down with a classic case of married man's guilt. That's the problem with strippers: they don't just take your dough, they also make you feel like the worst husband in the world the next morning. And if you think strippers are bad, by the way, try *groupies*: I used to get so out of my mind with guilt, I'd be down the doctor's office every day of the week, thinking I had some new disease. Then I'd finally break down, tell Sharon everything, and I'd get a houseplant over the back of my head, which meant another visit to the doctor's. As for the good old herpes: your GP will give you a test to see if you've got it, but the virus can lie dormant for years, so there'd be no telling if it was from the stripper or, say, an unwashed glass you picked up in a pub. I used to get outbreaks myself when I was stressed out or tired, but I haven't had any for years. One thing I wouldn't recommend is confessing to your missus. Believe me, it'll only make your life worse.

Dear Dr. Ozzy:
Out of the blue, my husband has suggested bringing another woman into our bedroom, to liven things a bit up after twenty years of marriage. I'm not keen. What do you think?
Susan, Dundee

Sounds fair enough to me—as long as what's good for the goose is good for the gander. If your husband gets to bring

Debbie from accounts to bed, then you should be able to bring along Dave from marketing. But that raises the obvious fucking question: if you both want to sleep with other people in your own home, what are you still doing together?

Dear Dr. Ozzy:
I've noticed that I can't last as long in bed with my girlfriend as I could when we first started going out with each other three months ago. Now I'm worried that if I don't fix this, she might leave me for someone who can fully please her. Any advice?
Ethan [no address given]

Send her to me! Seriously though, Ethan, this kind of thing is a big problem when you're a rock star. I remember one time when me and the guys from Black Sabbath were staying at a Holiday Inn in America, *three* groupies came to my room— one after the other. You'd have to be superhuman not to run out of steam during a session like that, especially after number two (and it's not like there was any Viagra around in those days). Fortunately I was a young man, so I activated the Special Reserve Tank and finished the job. But you've gotta bear in mind: that was just *one* wild night, which ain't exactly the same as a long-term relationship. When it goes to a steady girlfriend, it's natural that things simmer down a bit over time. Wait until you're married: you'll be in and out within five minutes while your missus is still doing the crossword.

Dear Dr. Ozzy:
A friend recently showed me some photos on his mobile of him boning a very hot girl. The problem is, the girl is a good friend of mine. Should I tell her what he's doing, or keep my mouth shut? I guess what I'm asking is, are you a "bros before hos" kinda guy?
Sean, New York

Send me the pictures and I'll decide. Seriously, though, this ain't a question of some bullshit code of male honor. If she's a friend, and you want her to stay your friend—tell her. Simple as that.

Dear Dr. Ozzy:
I'm 54 years old and sex mad. Does the lust ever fade?
Pete, Fife

If you're a red-blooded man, I firmly believe that the only time you'll ever get any peace from down below is when you're in the ground. Until then, the second brain below your waist is gonna be making its own decisions, whether you like it or not. I mean, I'm almost 62 years old, and I still love a good old game of "Where's the Salami?" Getting anyone to play it with me is another matter entirely. Luckily, as you get older, your memory goes, so if you see a sexy woman and start to feel randy, you can't remember what it was you were excited about five minutes later. That makes things a lot easier.

Dear Dr. Ozzy:
What's the nicest way to let a girl know she smells bad, especially, uh, y'know . . . "down there"?
Ron, Indiana

Try throwing up during sex. As they say, actions speak louder than words.

Dear Dr. Ozzy:
Is it ever acceptable for a married man to get a lap dance at a strip club?
Louise, Morecambe

If you're gonna tell your wife about it—*no*. If you're gonna NOT tell your wife about it—*yes*. But they're stupid places, strip clubs. I know people who spend most of their lives in them, like kids in a toy shop. I've never seen the attraction, personally. I mean, every female performer in a titty joint has been up close and personal with about ten other guys in the same night. How is that a turn-on? If someone's so desperate to see a pair of naked breasts, I suggest they buy a copy of *Playboy* and save themselves $500.

Dear Dr. Ozzy:
I'm a 28-year-old virgin (ouch). I recently met a girl and we tried to make love—but I couldn't finish. She accused me of indulging in solitary pleasures and wearing "the big chap" out. Is this possible? We tried again in the morning but my problems just got worse, and I couldn't even achieve match fitness. What's wrong with me?
Chris, Reading

This could just be nerves, Chris. Also, if you were drinking before your first attempt, that might have stopped you from reaching the fireworks ceremony. Then again, maybe you *are* "wearing the big chap out"—you don't exactly seem to be denying it, do you? So my advice to you is calm down, don't drink beforehand, and cut out the five-knuckle shuffles.

Dear Dr. Ozzy:
My husband—a builder—has always enjoyed it when I'm dominant in the bedroom, but the other day he asked me to call him a "good little girl" while we were making love. Should I be worried, or do all men have weird fantasies?
Jill, Huddersfield

Look, a lot of guys have strange things that get them going, but this one's a bit of cause for alarm, don't you think? I mean, if Sharon asked me to start calling her a "big bad boy" in the bedroom, I'd probably jump out the fucking window, screaming. Having said that, if you don't mind saying it, and he enjoys hearing it, then good luck to you both. Just make sure to keep a close eye on your underwear drawer, 'cos my guess is that when you leave the house in the morning your mister probably becomes a missus...

Dear Dr. Ozzy:

I'm in a serious relationship, but I've been thinking about going to one of those "rub'n'tug" massage parlours. Given that (a) my girlfriend will never know, (b) there's no chance of picking up an STD, and (c) it doesn't seem wrong, is there any reason I shouldn't?
"Jacob," Riverside, California

A handjob is a very personal thing, and after a lifetime of practise, most blokes get a pretty fucking specific preference for the kind of technique they like. So unless you're acting as a co-pilot and barking out instructions to your dodgy masseuse every two seconds, it might end up feeling more like she's skinning a dead rabbit than driving you wild with forbidden pleasure. In fact, it sounds to me like you've already built this up in your head to the point where it's gonna be an expensive disappointment. You also ain't factored in guilt. It's all very well you telling Dr. Ozzy that "it doesn't seem wrong" to hire an extra pair of hands to help out in the monkey-spanking department, but I'm afraid to say that if you're anything like me, your conscience won't agree.

IV: ROMANCE

Dear Dr. Ozzy:

My girlfriend bites my lip when we kiss. She thinks this is sexy, but actually it really hurts—it's so bad now, I try to avoid making out. How can I tell her this without hurting her feelings and/or looking like a wimp who can't take a bit of rough foreplay?
Giles, Fulham

Say to her: "If you're hungry, I'll get you a sandwich." Seriously, you ain't a wimp for not wanting to go to bed with Jaws every night. I've never understood people who get off on being in pain. I mean, life's hard enough as it is, so why turn the simple pleasure of getting your end away into something that involves ballgags and piano wire? Try biting her back, and see how *she* likes it. (If it turns her on, you might have a problem.)

Dear Dr. Ozzy:

My boyfriend hates all the television shows I watch, and when he criticises them (loudly and every night), it makes me feel like an idiot for wanting a bit of mindless distraction after a hard day at work. Does this mean I should break up with him?

Katy, Somerset

If couples broke up 'cos they didn't like the same kind of telly, the divorce rate would quadruple overnight. Men and women's brains are wired differently, so chances are, you ain't gonna want to watch a documentary on Gulf War tanks, and he ain't gonna want to watch some slurpy tear-jerker of a makeover show. You need to either take it in turns to watch your favourite shows; buy a second telly; or sit down, make a list of the stuff you both enjoy, and program the DVR accordingly. As for your boyfriend making you feel like an idiot—he probably just thinks he's as entitled to relax with something he enjoys after a hard day at work as you are. And I've gotta admit, I'm guilty of the same thing. I'm always saying to Sharon, "You ain't watching *that* fucking crap again, are you?!" Luckily there's always *one* thing on we both like: the news.

Dear Dr. Ozzy:

As a 30-year-old devout religious Roman Catholic virgin, I am finally considering playing the field until I find that special someone in my life. Is this morally and socially acceptable in the modern world?

Ryan, County Armagh

I think it's very admirable to hold out that long, 'cos it's so rare these days. At the same time, I have to say if I hadn't been laid by the time I was your age, I'd be asking myself, "What's wrong?"

I mean, I was 15 when I lost my virginity, and I was so randy, it felt like my underpants were about to explode. Another problem with holding out is that if you do finally marry someone, what happens if you discover that you don't like making love to them? You don't want to marry for lust, either—'cos you'll spend more time washing the dishes with your other half than you will between the sheets. So my prescription for you is to have one bonk, three times a day, for two weeks. Doctor's orders.

Dear Dr. Ozzy:
My girlfriend and I are talking about marriage. She's awesome, except for one thing: she gives the world's worst head. I mean, **really bad.** *Is this a good enough reason to move on and find another wife? A life of sub-par BJs seems like a life not worth living.*
"Guy," Colorado
    Look, I know blowjobs are quite nice, but life's not all about blowjobs. And there's always a tradeoff—for men *and* women. You could dump this girl and end up with a fiancé who's amazing at blowjobs but smells like a three-day-old fucking haddock. More important than that, Miss Fellatio USA might be a royal pain in the arse, never help around the house, and end up going down on your best mate while you're away on a business trip. Why not think of something you're girlfriend's *good* at, and concentrate on that?

Dear Dr. Ozzy,
I have a rather pushy, much older, single (unattractive) neighbour who has strongly hinted at us having a romantic relationship. I'm not interested in the slightest, but he's not getting the message, and every time I pass him in the street he races up to me. He's also started to become (inappropriately) touchy-feely. I don't want to fall out with him—he's my neighbour—but short of sprinting away when I see him, do I have any other option?
Katie (no address given)

It sounds to me like he's the kind of guy who won't give up no matter what you say, so if you've already tried the nice way, now's the time to tell him, "Look, what part of fuck off don't you understand?" I mean, no-one wants to fall out with their neighbour, but at the same time, you also don't want to be creeping out of your own front door, and diving into the hedgerow if you see him coming. Why should *you* have to live like that, when you're not the one with a problem? Make it clear: "There's no chance, there never will be a chance, and if you touch me again I'll take out a restraining order."

Dear Dr. Ozzy:

I've just finished college and moved back in with my mum ... but now I've developed feelings for her (younger) boyfriend, to the point where we flirt and hang out all the time. Should I come clean with my mom, or leave it alone? I didn't mean for this to happen!

Katy, Oklahoma

You do realize that it's every bloke's fantasy to get a mother *and* her daughter into the sack, don't you? Check out the internet if you don't believe me. I mean, if this guy gets into your pants after humping your mum, he's gonna be bragging about it for the rest of his life. If you're okay with that, sleep with him. If you'd rather have true love, then you should come clean about what's going on to your mum—and kick this creep out of the house.

DR. OZZY'S INCREDIBLY HELPFUL TIPS

Rules of Romance

◆ Guys: When trying to get your partner into the sack, avoid phrases like "meat thermometer," "one-eyed yogurt slinger," and "cheesy bratwurst." At least until you're married.

- ◆ Girls: they say a home-cooked meal is the way to man's heart. So are blowjobs, and they take a lot less time. You won't need a Jamie Oliver cookbook, either.
- ◆ Guys: *Always* pay. Or steal, and pretend you paid.* Women: always *offer* to pay, even if you'd dump the guy in a heartbeat if he made you do it.
- ◆ Both sexes: Make sure to buy little gifts for your partner at unexpected moments. That way, when you forget a birthday, you'll get less of a bollocking.

Dear Dr. Ozzy:
I finally married my girlfriend last year after a decade together. Now she wants kids (her clock is ticking!), but I'm terrified of the thought. What should I do?
Anonymous, USA

Get a dog. That should buy you a year or so. To be brutally honest, though, you should have thought about what she wanted before putting a ring on her finger. Now you've gotta be a man and live with the consequences. Who knows? Maybe you'll enjoy being a dad.

Dear Dr. Ozzy:
My girlfriend hasn't had sex with me for months—she's always too tired after work. Is our relationship dead? What can I do to make her interested in a game of hide-the-sausage?
Adam, Brooklyn

Romance, Adam. You need a bit of romance. That includes not using phrases like "hide the sausage." As I've always said to Sharon, there are 24 hours in a day, so it shouldn't be so hard to make sure you spend at least one of them with each

---

*Might not be legal where you live.

other. Go on a date. Have dinner together. Or put on a wig
and a false beard, check into a B&B, and shag the shit out of
each other, like you're having an affair. Maybe the fact she
isn't going to bed with you is a form of protest. Maybe she just
wants more excitement in her life.

Dear Dr. Ozzy:

*My boyfriend and I have split up a few times but keep getting
back together—we can't live apart! Recently, though, the
excitement we had six months ago has vanished (especially
for him). If ending it all isn't an option, how can we get the
spark back?*
Mary, Kent (17 years old)

Listen: at the age of 17, your excitement level is gonna be
going up and down like a fiddler's elbow. Just give it some
time. Most teenage relationships don't last. Then again, I've
also known people who met each other at your age and
lived happily ever after for the rest of their lives. (I've also
known people who lived together for ten years, got married,
then immediately got divorced.) The important thing is to
always be yourself. If your boyfriend doesn't find that exciting
enough, then believe me, he ain't worth the effort.

Dear Dr. Ozzy:

*After about a year of dating my girlfriend, I've finally realized that
I enjoy jerking off more than sleeping with her. Is this fucked up?
Should I break the news to her?*
"Scott," Connecticut

Let's face it: it's hard to beat a good old five-knuckle shuffle.
For a start, you don't have to take your right hand out for
dinner before it'll get down to business. It also doesn't care
if you last five minutes or five seconds—and it ain't gonna
demand an earth-shaking climax of its own. Admitting this

to your girlfriend is whole different thing, though. If she's anything like my own wife, I would advise against it—unless you want to be kicked so hard in the balls, you won't be able to knock one out again for the next ten years.

Dear Dr. Ozzy:

I have been with my beautiful wife for twenty years, and our sex life has always been wonderful—but instead of making love every day, like we used to, it's now just two or three times a week. I'm starting to worry if it's me or her—and if, as I'm getting older, my desire is fading (I'm 65). Please help, this is such a huge part of my life.

Howard, London

Three times a week—at the age of 65?! Come back to me when it's three times a year. Seriously, man...you ain't in a bad place. You need to enjoy yourself while you still can and stop moaning.

Dear Dr. Ozzy:

I'm a 42-year-old single man who lives with his mother. Worse than that, I'm a bedwetter. I'm convinced it's the reason why I've never had the confidence to ask a girl out on a date. Please help.

Terry, Lancaster

As I've said before, I used to be a bedwetter when I was still drinking. My wife Sharon would have to put on a life jacket when she went to sleep at night. It wasn't the just bed, either: I'd take a leak in the wardrobe, over the edge of the balcony, in the fridge-freezer, you name it. Eventually I went to my doctor and said, "Look, I don't want to p*** the bed, but I don't want to stop drinking." He told me, "You can have one or the other, but not both." So if you're a drinker: stop. In the meantime, go and see your GP. You ain't gonna tell him anything he ain't heard before, and this is worth checking out.

Dear Dr. Ozzy:

One of my old boyfriends (he dumped me) has just become engaged to a very wealthy, very good-looking, and very well-known French woman. I know it's not healthy, but I'm obsessing over it. In your experience, what's the best cure for a jealous heart?
Katherine, Rugby

You could always do what I did when I was dumped by a girl at Silver Blades ice rink in Birmingham: I got the word out to her friends that I was so upset, I was gonna emigrate to Australia (it was a ten-quid offer they were promoting in the travel agent's at the time). It was all bullshit: I didn't even have ten pennies in those days, never mind ten quid. But she had me back anyway. Then I realised I didn't like her that much to begin with. That's the funny thing with jealousy: it's not about wanting something 'cos it'll make you happy—it's about wanting something 'cos you've been told you can't have it.

Dear Ozzy,

My ex-boyfriend left me for my best friend last summer. Just to rub salt in the wound, I recently found out that he proposed a year to the day after breaking up with me. I'm now considering sending them a steaming bag of shit as a wedding gift. Should I do this, or let karma run its course?
Ashley, New Jersey

Think of it this way, Ashley: your steaming bag of shit IS his karma. Having said that, if you're gonna send crap in the mail, take a leaf out of my wife's book, and do it right: put it in a ziplock bag inside of a Tiffany's box. Everyone *loves* to get a Tiffany's box—which makes the thought of them untying the ribbon and bow to find a fresh dump inside even more satisfying.

Dear Dr. Ozzy:

A really good friend of mine went on a couple of dates with a very minor celebrity. Each time it felt like a **Bachelor** *episode,*

because he never made a move. Now, a month later—under a lot of pressure—he's confessed he has herpes. She still wants to date him, but in my opinion he can't be trusted. Who's right here?
Diana, California

Are you absolutely *sure* he has herpes? I might be wrong, but I don't think most guys would mention the H-word at all—especially not after two dates—unless they had a raging attack of it that was making their balls glow florescent green. To me, it seems like he might be using it as an excuse to cover up an even deeper secret. I mean, you never know: maybe he has a boyfriend on the side, and doesn't want to sleep with your friend at all.

Dear Dr. Ozzy,

I'm a heterosexual man—honestly—but found myself becoming stimulated in the most embarrassing way while getting a Swedish rub-down from a male masseuse. Even worse: it was a couple's massage, and my wife was lying next to me. She noticed, and hasn't talked to me since. What can I say to her to make this better?
Eric, Melrose

Oh, Eric. You could always say to your wife, "I've never kissed a man—but I might have kissed a man who has." Seriously, though ... I suppose the question is, would your wife have been more or less pissed off if you'd reacted in the same way to a female masseuse? If you think she might have been cooler with it, you could always tell her it was the thought of a *menage-a-trois* that set you off, not the big glistening hunk of love muscle who was stimulating your deep tissue. Actually, no, don't do that. All I can say is that in future, you might want to try avoiding other blokes when you're down the parlour. Personally, I couldn't think of anything more uncomfortable than being oiled down by some ex-Chippendale while Kenny G plays in the background. Don't get me wrong: I ain't got nothing against the gay community. But when someone says the word "Swedish" to me, I think Ingrid Bergman, not Bjorn Borg.

Dear Dr. Ozzy:

I'm still "friends with benefits" with my ex-boyfriend, even though he now has a new girlfriend—the same girl he cheated on me with for almost a year and a half. Should I tell her what the hell has been going on, since he hasn't had the balls to be honest?
Rudy, South Carolina

If you're looking for revenge, go ahead. But don't kid yourself—it sounds to me like this is a play to get him back. You might also want to consider that if he's cheated on you, and cheated on her, he's probably screwing a few other people, too. I mean, the bloke doesn't exactly sound like the faithful type. My advice would be to find a new guy and move on.

Dear Dr. Ozzy:

My girlfriend's father—Russian, ex-military—likes to get me drunk on vodka then take me to his banya (sauna) where we strip naked and he whips me with birch leaves. Is this weird?
Adam, New York

If some bird's dad ever tried to get me naked and start whipping me with something—birch or otherwise—he'd get a punch on the fucking nose. Getting boozed up in a sauna ain't a very clever idea, either... although I used to do it all the time at my old house in Staffordshire. I'd always take special precautions, mind you: before putting any water on the coals, I'd always top-off my lager with a splash of lemonade. A "lemonade top," we used to call it. (Not the same thing as a shandy, which is half-and-half.) One other thing, Adam: generally speaking, any kind of physical activity in hot, steamy conditions is best avoided, unless you're using the sauna to have a quickie with the nanny, which I once did, long ago. In that case, an exception can be made.

Dear Dr. Ozzy:
I wish my girlfriend were better endowed. Would it be rude to suggest a boob job? (I'd pay for it.)
Stan, Cheshire

The good thing about being Dr. Ozzy is that I sometimes get the opportunity to save lives. Stan, count yourself lucky, 'cos that's what I'm about to do: under NO circumstances EVER bring this up with your girlfriend. If I made this suggestion to Sharon, believe me, the Osbourne crown jewels would end up halfway up my oesophagus. And to be honest I wouldn't blame her. I mean, imagine if the situation was reversed, and your girlfriend asked you to get an enlargement of your own? How would *that* feel? If it's really that important to you, dump the girl and find yourself a Page 3 model.

Dear Dr. Ozzy,
What's the best way to make a woman sleep with you?
Jake, New York

I always had a great chat-line up for the women. After a night out, I'd say, "Can I come back to your house and watch your telly?" It was brilliant, 'cos it made it sound like all I wanted to do was catch up on the *News at Ten*, when in fact I was planning to get them into the sack. No-one ever fell for it, though. Most of the time they just went, "I ain't got a telly."

III: BALLCARE

Dear Dr. Ozzy:
This might sound strange, but I've noticed that when I stare at my testicles for a long time, they seem to move by all themselves . . . is this normal? It's freaking me out!
Jason (13 years old), Kent

It's normal. If they start moonwalking, you might have a problem... but they definitely move on their own, 'cos they're surrounded by a layer of jelly and, as everyone knows who's looked at a bowl of jelly before, it tends to wobble around a lot for no good reason. On a separate note: you might want to spend less time staring at your testicles.

Dear Dr. Ozzy:
The skin on my penis has cracked due to (solo) over-use. Is this normal? If so, how can I make it heal?
Anonymous, New York
It's called friction. Rub the skin on your elbow ten times a day and you'll have exactly the same problem. Give your Upstanding Citizen a break for a while, then invest in some lubrication.

Dear Dr. Ozzy:
I've been contacted by a very friendly woman on the internet who tells me that "male enhancement" surgery—ie, phalloplasty— is risk-free and guaranteed to make me a hero in bed. Should I proceed?
Larry, California
No. Next question...

Dear Dr. Ozzy:
I'm an uncircumcised 16 year old and can't retract my foreskin. I'm stressing out about it, but can't face going to a doctor (which would mean telling my parents). What can I do?
Mark, Birmingham
First of all, under no circumstances start messing around with it yourself. Second: I appreciate that it's embarrassing, but the best thing to do is have a quiet word with your dad, or if you've got one, an older brother. Bear in mind that your old man probably changed a few of your nappies when you were little, so

you ain't showing him anything he hasn't seen a million times already. The same goes for your doctor: believe me, people have far worse problems than a sticky foreskin (which has gotta be pretty common). Just pluck up the courage and get it over with, 'cos it'll seem like nothing as soon as it's done.

DR. OZZY'S AMAZING MEDICAL MISCELLANY

What Every Man Should Know...

- "Blue balls" is a *real* condition. It's a kind of cramp that happens when you have a woody for a long time but never get to the fireworks ceremony. Another interesting fact: no female in medical history has *ever* accepted "blue balls" as a reason for a bonk.
- The average guy gets an average of five boners every night. If the average guy is anything like me, he also gets an average of zero shags.
- One ejaculation contains up to 400 million sperm. I'm guessing it was a woman who counted 'em, 'cos the bloke would have been fast asleep.
- With quick treatment, the survival rate for testicular cancer is about 95 percent. The trick is to check your balls regularly for lumps. Don't do it during business meetings or at dentists' appointments, though.

Dear Dr. Ozzy:
I've heard that regular ejaculations are important to keep the prostate healthy as one gets older. As there is a history of prostate cancer in my family, would a regular "cleaning out of the system" be a good idea, purely from a health point of view? If so, how often?
Andy, Beaconsfield

You're absolutely right, Andy. I recommend a vigorous spring cleaning once a day. It's best done in private, but if you're caught, mention the words "preventative medicine" and you'll be fine.

Dear Dr. Ozzy:

I saw a yellow spongy froth come out of my 54-year-old boyfriend's penis during ejaculation. He says it's been three years since he had sex. Could it be "rusty pipes"? I'm a 38-year-old woman, and I've seen a lot—but I've never seen that before!

Haydee, Fleetwood, New York

Listen, Haydee: If I had yellow spongy frothy shit coming out of my dick, I wouldn't be writing to Dr. Ozzy—I'd be running to the fucking hospital! It's a cause for alarm, don't you think? It reminds me of when I was younger, and this school friend of mine started to piss sperm. You ain't never seen anything like it. We were all looking at him, our jaws on the floor, going, "Is this what happens when you reach 13? Is that his life supply—*gone*?" I've no idea what happened to that kid, but I hope he got it checked out. But back to your question: you could always get your boyfriend to knock a few out by himself, to see if the problem really is "rusty pipes," but, personally, I'd be making a date with my local dick doctor—and not wasting any time about it, either.

Dear Dr. Ozzy:

Do men really suffer "shrinkage" in their private area after going swimming (especially in cold water)? If so, what sort of percentage reduction is normal—50 per cent? More?

Felicity, Muswell Hill

Yes, shrinkage is very real, and very upsetting. I don't know about the percentage, though: I've never thought to get out my slide rule and calculator when it's happened to me. Also, in case you're wondering, hot water doesn't have the reverse effect—otherwise you'd see guys walking around with electric kettles swinging from their underpants.

Dear Dr. Ozzy:
I've decided I don't want any more kids, so I've asked my doc to give me the snip. Good idea?
David, Edinburgh

There are a lot of ways to avoid having kids that don't involve surgery. Also, the thing you've gotta remember about a vasectomy is that you can't undo it—well, you *can*, but it ain't easy. I'm speaking from experience here: in the 1980s, whenever I came back from a tour, I'd get Sharon pregnant, to the point when she had our three kids—Aimee, Kelly, and Jack—in three years on the trot. She'd had enough of being the size of a semi-detached house by then, so I went to my doc and told him to get out his sharpest pair of scissors and do what was necessary. The op was fine, although I had a bit of swelling afterwards ("Doc, can you make it *not* go away," I said). The real problem came a few weeks later, when Sharon got all broody again. So I had to go back to the doc and ask him to unsnip me. "I wish you lot would bloody make your minds up!" he said to me. Anyway, whatever it was he did to glue my tubes back together obviously didn't work, 'cos there weren't any more little Osbournes after that.

Dear Dr. Ozzy:
Last month I noticed that in my right testicle, there seem to be two "balls" instead of one. I don't have any pain, though—should I see my GP?
Saif, London

Yes, *immediately*. It could be something, or it could be nothing—but if you feel any kind of strange lump in your balls, you can't ignore it, because it could be life-threatening. Testicular cancer is a lot more common than you'd think. A good friend of mine had it: they put some of his man-juice in a jar—in case he wanted to have kids later—got the scissors of doom out, then gave him a blast of chemo, just to be on the safe side. I'm not trying to be funny, 'cos it ain't. And I'm not saying you've got cancer, either. But in a case like this, don't mess around, man. Forget Dr. Ozzy. Go and see a real doctor.

Dear Dr. Ozzy:
I'm pretty sure I have a much-smaller-than-average penis. As a result, I'm scared of talking to girls and am thinking of getting enlargement surgery. Is this a good idea?
Hugh, New Mexico

Look, if it ain't broke, don't try to fix it—'cos the only thing worse than a very small penis is a very small penis that shoot blanks and looks like some mutant fucking eel from outer space. I mean, just think of the shit that could go wrong, man. Those plastic surgeon guys couldn't even get Michael Jackson's face right, so why would you entrust them with your *dick*? I certainly wouldn't believe the ads they send you on e-mail. Believe me: if that stuff really worked, there'd be lines around the block. My advice? Steer clear.

Dr. Ozzy's Trivia Quiz: Sexy Beast

Find the answers—and tote up your score—on page 263

1. If your partner has a headache before sex, what's the best natural cure?
   a) A game of hide-the-sausage
   b) An early night and plenty of sleep
   c) A neck massage

2. If a girl has a fling with a guy who says he has diphallia, what should she expect between the sheets?
   a) Delayed ejaculation
   b) A "micropenis"
   c) Double the pleasure

3. When a 22-year-old student from California auctioned her virginity in 2009, how much did she get?
   a) $50,000
   b) A packet of fags and a box of Maltesers
   c) $3.8 million

4. During the "Honen Matsuri" festival in Japan, what do 12 men carry through the streets?
   a) A naked woman
   b) A 96-inch wooden schlong
   c) A ceremonial bowl of human sperm

5. A bloke in the Wodaabe tribe of Central Africa will find a wife by...
   a) Putting on a skirt and taking part in a beauty contest
   b) Arm-wrestling the potential bride's father
   c) Showing the size of his woody to the town's elders

The Pharmacology Section

11

What They Don't Print on the Label

I might know fuck all about molecules, equations, or the periodic table, but I do know something about chemicals—mainly 'cos I was off my nut on them for the best part of 40 years. Things have changed a lot since my junkie days, though. Back in the 1970s, for example, you needed a dodgy dealer and a wad of cash to get your hands on any mind-altering substances. These days, it's all *legal*. As long as you've got a prescription, it's considered perfectly acceptable to be stoned out of your mind 24 hours a day, 7 days a week. The problem is, people are happy to empty all these jars of pills down their neck without ever reading the labels—probably 'cos the warnings are all written by lawyers and say crazy things like, "Side-effects might include DEATH." That's where Dr. Ozzy comes in. If you want a straight answer about a medication, why not ask someone who's taken *everything*?

Just bear in mind, though: before putting any drug in your body—even if it's completely legit—you should always talk to someone first who *didn't used to be in Black Sabbath*. As for all those people who are still using illegal drugs in one way or the other, all I can say is, "Been there, done that, and I honestly pray to God I never go back there again." I mean, yeah, some of it was fun at the time. So is driving your car at 150 mph on the wrong side of the road. The trouble is, sooner of later, there'll be an 18-wheeler coming round the corner in the opposite direction. And that won't be any fun at all.

I: UPPERS

Dear Dr. Ozzy:
I work at a high-energy law firm and recently got myself a prescription for Adderall to boost my work performance. Thing is, I'm totally not ADD. Is this cheating at life?
Anonymous

It really depends how much you're taking. If you're necking a handful of the stuff a time, then you might as well go to work on a gram of fucking cocaine. And as time goes by, you'll get a tolerance to it, and you'll have to keep taking more and more, until you end up sitting there in your cubicle with your eyes bugging out like a fucking nutter and clutching at your chest every five seconds, 'cos you think you're about to have a heart attack. That ain't cheating at life—that's fast-tracking yourself to an early death. Personally, I have a genuine case of ADD, but I give my Adderall to my assistant Tony, otherwise I'd be pouring the stuff in my coffee and sprinkling it on my cornflakes. The fact that you're even writing to me about this suggests you know you've got a problem.

Dear Dr. Ozzy:

I suspect that my brother has started to take cocaine when he goes out clubbing at the weekend. I'm terribly worried about him. What are the risks involved?
Susan, West Yorks

You're right to worry. When you start taking heavy-duty amounts of cocaine, this white gunk starts to trickle down the back of your throat, and you find yourself doing that phlegm-clearing thing all the time: like a sniff, but deeper and gunkier. And that puts a lot of stress on your epiglottis, or "clack," as I've always called it. When I was doing a lot of coke in the 1970s, I was clearing away phlegm so often, I ended up tearing my clack in half. I was lying in bed at the time, and I just felt it flop down inside the back of my throat. Then it swelled up to the size of a golf ball and I had to go to the doc and explain myself. Luckily he had some pills for it—but I was so paranoid from the coke, I thought I'd never sing again. So as much fun as your brother might be having now, Susan, I'd advise him to stop while he's ahead, 'cos a coke habit never ends well.

Dear Dr. Ozzy:

I recently went to Brazil and saw the most unbelievably graphic health warnings on the back of cigarette packets—dead babies, gangrenous feet, amputees, etc. Do you think these kind of "scare tactics" work, or are they so over-the-top, they do the opposite?
Don, Greenwich

The fact that anyone can puff and cough their way through a packet of smokes while staring at a picture of a foot-wide throat tumour just goes to show how addictive those fucking things are. I swear, if someone invented nicotine today, it would be in the same class as heroin—and I say that as someone's whose smoked cigarettes AND taken heroin. I remember being so hooked on tobacco, I'd pick butts up off the floor and smoke them. Disgusting, man. The thing is, though, when they start printing those kind of horrific pictures on the cartons—like kids' corpses and whatever—you've gotta ask yourself, why the hell are they selling that shit in the first place? At some point they've either gotta ban the things or let people get on with killing themselves.

Dear Dr. Ozzy,

My 46-year-old son inherited an addictive personality from his father (who was a big drinker), and has somehow ended up with a crack habit. Worse: when I went away on holiday recently, he burgled my house for drug money, leaving his DNA all over the place. I feel terrible. Why do you think he's doing this? Is it a cry for help?

Jeanette, Coventry

You answered your own question at the very beginning— no, it's not a cry for help, your son is an *addict*. He just wants his drug. It's as simple as that. A lot of people might find it hard to believe, but addiction is an illness, similar to having any other kind of mental disorder, and no-one can really help you until you decide for yourself that it's time to pack it in. That ain't much comfort when the person who used to be your little angel takes up the crackpipe, though. The first thing I'd do is sit him down and tell him you know exactly what the deal is. Then give one last chance: "I can help you get over this, or I can let the police handle it, and you can go to prison." If he wants your support, find a helpline or a drugs counselling service and take it from there. If he wants to be a crackhead, there ain't much you can do. At this point, tough love is the only option.

OZZY'S AMAZING MEDICAL MISCELLANY

Up, Up and Away

◆ Back in the 1880s, an American doc called William Halsted realised that if you shot yourself up with cocaine, it worked like an anaesthetic. Unfortunately it also makes you a raging fucking coke-head—which is why you don't get to snort a line before having your appendix out. The guy ended up trying to cure his own habit with morphine...which just made him a coke head *and* a smack-head.

◆ Sigmund Freud recommended cocaine as a treatment for depression, alcoholism, morphine addiction...and just about anything else he could think of. Mind you, coke was all the rage back then. You could even get bottles of "cocaine wine"—one of the greatest inventions in the history of Mankind. The drink was taken off the market in 1886, though, 'cos of prohibition. So they replaced it with a non-alcoholic version...called "Coca-Cola." Six years later, the cocaine was taken out, too.

◆ During World War II, soldiers on all sides were speeding their balls off half the time—until generals realised that there's no point being able to march 300 miles in five minutes if you spend the next week bugging the fuck out from paranoia. If you believe some reports, even Hitler was taking methamphetamine eight times a day.

◆ Speaking of meth, it's gotta be one of the scariest fucking "uppers" of all time—even though in the 1940s, it was approved as a treatment for everything from hay fever to narcolepsy. One of the worst side-effects is "meth mouth," which causes your teeth to turn black and fall out. To make the stuff, meanwhile, labs use everything from brake cleaner to laptop batteries, fertilizer, cat litter and road flares. It ain't exactly "organic," put it that way.

Dr. Dr. Ozzy:

Are energy drinks mixed with booze a safer (and legal) alternative to cocaine?

Lizzy, London

Good question, but I don't know the answer, 'cos whenever I drank energy drinks with booze, I was on cocaine, too. As an addict, it's all the fucking same. Y'know, if people like messing themselves up, fine—but it didn't end well for me. One thing I will say is that when addicts give up the booze and drugs, caffeine is often the only thing left for them to take. I've heard of people mixing Diet Coke and Red Bull and topping up their glass throughout the day. You see those same guys at AA meetings, huddled around the coffee machine, twitching. It's sad, man. But the most unnatural thing for any addict is to *not* be getting high. Anything will do. I suppose I'm lucky that I've got music to take my mind off things. And my family, and my 17 precious dogs . . . and my English tea.

Dear Dr. Ozzy:

How did you manage to quit smoking? I've tried everything: patches, gum, cold turkey, and pills, but it isn't working for me. It's driving me insane. Please tell me your secret—and remember, not all of us have the money for fancy doctors!

Greg, USA

It's simple: you've gotta make your mind up. I'd stop, I'd start, I'd stop again, I'd put the patch on, take the patch off, put it on again, smoke *with* the patch, stop again, try the gum, smoke with the patch *and* the gum...I even tried hypnosis at one point. I loved smoking. Cigarettes, pipes, cigars—anything. I smoked so much I set my house on fire on more than one occasion. For a while I used to roll my own: I'd make 25 in one go, put them in a box, and smoke 'em through the night. I couldn't go for a walk without a cigarette, make a call without a cigarette, do *anything* without a cigarette. Then one day I had a conversation with myself: "Do you really want to stop, Ozzy, or do you want to keep going? You can't do both, so make a fucking decision." What swung it for me is the fact that I'm a singer: if I wanted to carry on entertaining people I had to quit. So one day I went home, threw my pack on the fire, and I've never smoked since. That was eight years ago. I don't crave them any more, but every so often I'll have a twinge. I just let it go, y'know? Because I ain't under any illusions: if I have just one cigarette now, I'll have smoked my way through an entire packet by the end of the day.

I: DOWNERS

Dr. Dr. Ozzy:
When I drink too much, the next morning I get a super-sensitive boner. Have you ever heard of this?
Bill, Georgia

No. With the amount I used to put away, I was lucky to even know I had a dick the next morning, never mind a boner. I also had a habit of waking up in jails and hospitals, which doesn't exactly put you in the mood. The only thing that was super-sensitive was my head.

Dear Dr. Ozzy:
I've recently been prescribed some medication that says "avoid alcohol," but both my consultant and my GP say it's okay to drink

"in moderation." They don't say what "moderation" is, though.
What's your opinion, as a man with a fair bit of experience?
Henry, Cambridgeshire

Here's my prescription for you, Henry: a new consultant, and a new GP. I mean, who are these people—witch doctors? If the manufacturer of the drug goes to all the bother of putting a big yellow label on the front which says "AVOID ALOCHOL," then—here's a crazy idea—how about *avoiding* alcohol? It ain't complicated. Y'know, I can't believe doctors sometimes. I think the problem is that docs like to knock a few back themselves. I had this one bloke in London, and every time I went into his surgery, the place stank of gin, his nose glowed bright red, and he chained-smoked while he scribbled down his dodgy prescriptions in a little pad. I stopped going to see him in the end. I felt worse coming out of there than I did when I went in.

Dear Dr. Ozzy:
My doctor has prescribed Vicodin for a degenerative disc problem in my back, but my physical therapists say I should find an alternative besides narcotics. What do you think?
Bob, Georgia

I was hooked on that shit for a long time. Vicodin and me were made for each other—*I love it.* Especially Vicodin ES (for Extra Strength). But trust me, when you're hooked on Vicodin, it's almost fucking impossible to kick. I was popping 25 a day at one point, and that's very dangerous, 'cos Vicodin is cut with stuff that can be extremely bad for your liver. Having said that, if you take Vicodin as your doctor prescribes it, you should be okay. If it says "take one every 6 hours" on the bottle, that's what you've got to do. With me, I'd end up taking 6 every *one* hour, and blame it on my dyslexia. So you need to decide if you trust yourself. Or, if you think you need the meds and you *don't* trust yourself, give the bottle to a relative or friend, so it ain't within easy reach.

DR. OZZY'S AMAZING MEDICAL MISCELLANY

Don't Get Me Down

◆ Alcohol is basically a downer, even though it can make you do crazy hyperactive shit if you drink enough of it. That's 'cos it reduces activity in the brain and central nervous system—the same thing that barbiturates, benzodiazepines, and modern sleeping medications like Zolpidem do.

◆ Barbiturates have long been used as "truth serums" by psychiatrists and the military—mainly thanks to an American doc, William Blackwenn, who discovered the benefits of "narcoanalysis" in the 1930s. Meanwhile, the Russians are thought to have a secret truth drug called SP-117 with no taste, no smell, no colour, and no obvious side-effects.

◆ Mixing downers with uppers might seem like a brilliant idea at 11pm on a Saturday night, but the U.S. Food and Drug Administration doesn't agree: in 2010, it told the makers of Four Loko—nicknamed "blackout in a can"—to stop mixing caffeine and booze. The up/down combination leaves you "wide-awake drunk," according to some experts, meaning you don't realise how pissed you're getting. Irish coffee is still legal, though...

◆ Another downer is chloral hydrate—which became famous when a Chicago bartender, Mickey Finn, was accused of spiking his customer's drinks with it in 1903 (so he could rob 'em when they passed out). That's why if you're drugged in a bar it's known as being "slipped a Mickey." I bought some chloral hydrate myself once: it came in little gel caps and worked great on overly aggressive fans.

Dear Dr. Ozzy:

To numb pain in my lower back, I've been "chipping" with heroin—ie, only doing it once every few days. But I'm getting scared, because now I'm counting the hours until I can do it again. I'm not stupid: I know what smack can do to people. But I also hate people's attitudes to it. They'll skip off to the bathroom for a few lines of cocaine—just as destructive!—yet would be shocked at my smoking heroin (I don't inject). If you could give me any advice, I would very much appreciate it.
Zadie, Glasgow

This ain't a good idea. I've seen the same thing happen so many times: you start "chipping"; then the smoking becomes more regular; then all of a sudden it's not enough, and it leads straight to the needle. I've lost so many good friends because of that. Also: when you take street heroin—unlike an opiate that's been prescribed by a doctor—you don't know what you're getting, man. I tried street heroin twice in my life, and it made me violently sick. You've also got to realise that it takes a lot of special training to administer heavy-duty pain drugs. That's why hospitals have anaesthesiologists. I know it can be difficult to get pills from a doctor, but if you have a genuine condition, it shouldn't be a problem. If you're anything like me, you're probably using your back pain as an excuse. Either way, find a GP or an addiction clinic—and be honest with 'em. There's a lot of help out there, and you don't have much time to lose.

Dear Dr. Ozzy:

I'm thinking of giving up booze. Does beer count?
Antony, Bristol

The first rule of alcoholism is that beer doesn't count. Neither does vodka, wine, cognac, scotch, gin . . . Unfortunately when you realise you don't want to be an alcoholic any more, *everything* counts. That's why you can't touch a drop. Anything else is a deal with the devil, and you'll only ever lose.

Dear Dr. Ozzy:

My teenage daughter, who is half-Chinese, suffers from red flushes when she drinks alcohol—a common complaint for her ethnicity. But she says that if she takes a stomach acid tablet just before she goes out, it can be controlled. Is this dangerous, do you think?

Anonymous, Berkshire

So let me get this straight, Mr. Anonymous from Berkshire: you're worried about the stomach acid tablet...but not the booze? Well, here's a little secret: I've been thrown in jail more times than I can remember; I've almost died on a number of other occasions; and I once tried to kill my own wife. None of this happened because of Pepto Bismol.

Dear Dr. Ozzy:

I live in Southern California and have been prescribed legal "medical marijuana" (for muscle pain), but it's making me paranoid. How can I reduce this side-effect—and what do you think of the claimed link between pot and schizophrenia?

Lisa, Los Angeles

When I used to smoke pot, it was happy stuff: you'd get the munchies, have a laugh, and go to sleep. These days, when you have a joint, you end up holding onto your drawers and hoping you don't go insane. I don't know about the link with schizophrenia, but I do know that they fuck around with marijuana now, creating all these genetically altered mutant varieties. In the old days, a joint's THC content—the chemical that gets you high, basically—used to be something like 4 per cent. Today, you hear of it being 20 per cent or even 40 per cent. It's a bit like walking into a bar one day and being given a Bud Light, and the next being given something likes looks exactly like a Bug Light, and tastes exactly like a Bud Light, but which has the same effect on you as four bottles of vodka. As for reducing your paranoia: back in the 1970s, the way to do it was to have a beer.

It didn't work, though. It just made you drunk *and* paranoid.

Dear Dr. Ozzy:

In your opinion, which alcoholic beverage delivers the least unpleasant hangover—ie, red wine versus vodka or beer? As the festive season approaches, I'd like to indulge in the seasonal merriment, while making the mornings-after bearable.
Rod, Canterbury

You're asking me the wrong question. Trying to cure your hangover while you're still drinking ain't gonna have a happy ending, no matter what kind of booze you avoid. Alcohol is Alcohol. If you drink enough of it, nothing on the planet can save you. And after the third glass, any rule you've made up for yourself before you started to get slaughtered is gonna go straight out of the window. So the only thing you can really do is treat the hangover. Now, over the years, I developed a fail-safe cure for the morning-after. Basically, I'd mix four tablespoons of brandy with four tablespoons of port, throw in some milk, a few separated eggs, and—if I was in a festive mood—some nutmeg. Then I'd mix it up and down it the second I woke up. The way it works is very clever: it gets you *instantly* blasted again, so you don't feel a thing. The only problem? Unless you keep drinking, the hangover that eventually catches up with you is about a thousand gazillion times worse than it would have been otherwise.

Dear Dr. Ozzy:

I'm a heavy boozer and now I get pains in my side quite often when I drink. I still have my appendix, both kidneys, and of course my liver. Which organ is the problem, do you think?
Kyle, British Columbia

I had the exactly same thing, and it turned out to be a damaged nerve from my kidneys to my liver. It was a big relief, to be honest with you, 'cos I was shitting myself that I had cirrhosis—I've lost many a good friend to that disease, and it ain't a pretty way to go, believe me. If you're gonna persist in drinking, my advice is to get regular blood tests, to see if your liver and kidneys are still holding up. Even better: quit altogether. I'll never forget what happened to this guy Mickey I used to know. He was told by his doctor to stop boozing, so he went straight to the pub for his last pint, took one sip, and dropped stone dead, right there at the bar. Whatever you do, don't end up like him.

Dear Dr. Ozzy:
I'm considering using Rohypnol—the "Date Rape Drug"—as a relaxant. Is this wise?
Catherine, Newcastle

I tried it in Germany a few years back. I'd gone to see this guy to buy some sleeping pills, but he was sold out, so he asked if I wanted to try some Rohypnol instead. Now, as it happened, I'd heard all about Rohypnol: the press was going crazy about it at the time, calling it the "date-rape drug," but I thought it was all bullshit. A drug that could completely paralyse you while you remained fully awake? It seemed too good to be true. So I bought a couple of doses of the stuff and decided to try it out—my own little science experiment. I gulped down the pills with a nip of booze as soon as I got back to my hotel room. Then I waited. "Well, this is a load of bollocks," I said to myself. Then two minutes later—while I was lying on the edge of the bed, trying to order a movie on the telly with the remote control—it suddenly kicked in. I couldn't move...*but I was wide awake!* It was the weirdest feeling, man. The only trouble was that I'd been dangling on the edge of the bed when my muscles seized up, so I ended up sliding to the floor and whacking my head on the coffee table on the way down. It hurt like fuck. I spent five hours trapped between the bed and the radiator, unable to move or talk.

So I can't say I recommend it.

Dear Dr. Ozzy:

I've been drinking heavily for a few years now, and find myself turning redder and redder. What can I do?

Jim, Devon

I looked like Rudolph the Alcoholic Reindeer by the end of my drinking days. They say blueberries can help. In my experience, though, not being off your nut 24 hours a day is a safer bet.

Dear Dr. Ozzy:

I'm 72 years old and have been taking Temazepam for tinnitus for a number of years (without any side effects), but I've decided recently that I'd like to come off the medication. I was going to go "cold turkey," but your comments about the trouble you had coming off sleeping pills have frightened the living daylights out of me! What should I do?

Debbie, Lancaster

The most important thing to do is talk to whoever gave you the prescription. Temazepam is a very powerful drug, so don't listen to the Prince of Darkness (or anyone else) until you've had a professional opinion. For what it's worth, it took me a year and a half to get off the same stuff. You go through *hell*. The problem is that the drugs make you used to sleeping artificially, so the withdrawal is evil. You have to do it very, *very* slowly. At 72, if you ain't having any side-effects, ask yourself if it's really worth the trouble.

Dear Dr. Ozzy:

Is it true that if you drink a pint of milk before going on the booze—to "line your stomach"—you can avoid a hangover?

Gareth, Durham

I used to have a similar hangover cure, but it involved putting booze in the milk. The fact is, everyone who drinks too much has these ridiculous old wives' tales, but there's only one medically proven way to avoid a hangover: don't fucking drink in the first place. If you want to have a pint of milk *and* a hangover, fine, but don't kid yourself into thinking a glass of semi-skimmed before a heavy night is gonna do any good. That's bullshit.

Dear Dr. Ozzy:

A friend of mine was hit by a car during his teens, and he's never been quite the same since. We've both now developed a taste for high-strength weed, but I've now realised that it makes him crazy and delusional (he says he's slept with Lady Gaga). He was put in care for a while, but as soon as he got out he went back to the dope. All my friends have tried telling him to stop, but it just makes him violent. What should I do?

Anonymous

You can't *make* anyone do anything—but you can say to your friend, "Look, I'm here if you ever want me help." What I've realised is, there are some who can have one joint every so often and be perfectly happy with that, and there are some who can't. For me, I started with weed, and ended up on heroin. A lot of people also make the mistake of thinking weed is harmless, but they should ask themselves the question: if you were gonna have open-heart surgery, and you had the choice between a doctor who'd just smoked a couple of joints, and a doctor who was clean, which one would you choose?

Dear Dr. Ozzy:

Here in Denmark, people believe you can get drunk by bathing your feet in tub of vodka, as the skin absorbs the booze in the same way as the lining of your stomach. Is this true?

Henrick, Copenhagen

Yes and no. I tried it once, but got bored after a few minutes and started drinking from the tub. The next morning, I wasn't sure if it was my feet or my mouth that had given me the hangover.

III: PYSCHADELICS

Dear Dr. Ozzy:
I've been taking a lot of LSD recently, mostly because the fake reality is better than my bummer of a real life. Have you ever felt the same way?
Anonymous, USA

Here's the deal, no bullshit: if you keep taking the LSD, your "fake reality" will soon become a lot fucking worse than real life, no matter how bad your real life is. In my experience, LSD is a great time until it ain't—and when that happens, it's the worst thing that's ever happened to you. One minute you're running down Miami Beach with a foam finger on your head; the next you're sticking a gun in your best friend's face. The worst thing is when you want the trip to stop, but you've still got another eight hours to go. I still get the after-effects of LSD to this day: I call them my "wobblers." In a flash, every tiny little problem freaks me out and becomes the end of the world. Seriously, man, be very careful. If you keep taking that shit, it's gonna bite you on the balls.

Dear Dr. Ozzy:
I've heard people say LSD can cure depression. What's your expert medical opinion on this?
Brian, Seattle

As I've said before, I wouldn't recommend that anyone take acid. On the other hand, it does open your mind to certain things. For example, I once walked into a field in Staffordshire when I was as high on LSD and ended up having a long conversation with a cow. After a while, the cow turned to the cow next to it and said, "FUCK me—that bloke can *talk*."

OZZY'S AMAZING MEDICAL MISCELLANY

Turn On, Tune In ... Freak OUT

- As crazy as it sounds, LSD is making a comeback as a possible treatment for everything from "cluster headaches" to post-combat stress. After a 40-year ban on government-funded research, the US Food and Drug Administration is allowing trials again. LSD is still illegal and dangerous, though, so it ain't a good idea to attempt any experiments of your own.

- Ask any major acid-head about "Bicycle Day" and he'll know exactly what you're talking about—it was the afternoon in 1943 when the Swiss chemist Albert Hofmann mistakenly took 100 times the "threshold dose" of LSD and then tried to ride home from his lab on a bicycle. Needless to say, the journey took a long time and involved visiting several other universes. Before then, no-one knew how high you could get from LSD (which is made from lysergic acid, found in certain kinds of fungi).

- No matter how much more research they do into LSD, it ain't likely to become a new blockbuster drug any time soon, 'cos it was discovered such a long time ago. That means all the chemical formulas behind it are now "in the public domain" and aren't gonna make anyone rich.

- Other common psychedelic drugs include peyote (a small, spineless cactus which contains mescaline), psilocybin (found in certain kinds of "magic" mushrooms) and PCP—which was used as an anaesthetic until surgeons realised it gave their patients head-trips that were worse than their injuries. Illegal PCP later became known as "angel dust."

Dear Dr. Ozzy:

After spending the late sixties and the seventies in a psychedelic fog, I've found that even now, after thirty years of abstinence, my sight hasn't recovered. Everything moves or breathes—the walls, the floors, people's faces—and I can wake up in the night with full-on "acid vision." Do you suffer from this? If so, what can I do about it?

Phil, Aberystwyth

They used to tell you that LSD never leaves your system for the rest of your life, although I think that's been disproven now. What might be happening is that something's triggering a memory of a bad trip—like when you think about spicy food and your mouth starts to water. But it doesn't sound very fucking normal, still having "acid vision" after 30 years. You should go and get an MRI, because you never know, it might not even have anything to do with the crazy shit you took when you were a younger man.

IV: EVERYTHING ELSE

Dear Dr. Ozzy:

Was Charlie Sheen really "winning" when he was fired from **Two and a Half Men?** *Or is it impossible to lead such a wild existence without some kind of tragic conclusion?*

Ted, Yorkshire

There are three things I don't like talking about these days: religion, politics, and Charlie Sheen. I'll say this, though: if Charlie Sheen had found a cure for cancer, the guy wouldn't have got as much press as he did when he was doing his Winning Warlock thing—which probably says more about our society than it does him. Also, as a general rule, it ain't ever a good idea to make a big announcement about how you're suddenly clean and sober, 'cos chances are, you'll fall off the wagon at some point—and I guarantee, there'll be a camera there, waiting for you. Been there, done that, got the T-shirt, the baseball cap, the mug and spoon set, and every other souvenir you can think of.

Dear Dr. Ozzy:

I am a 47-year-old woman who's indulged in various medicinal herbs and chemicals for most of my life. Now I'd like to stop, but how do I fight the urge to self-medicate?
Lucille, New York

It ain't easy. When I finally admitted that I had a problem with booze, my mum said to me, "Well why don't you just stop bloody *drinking then?*" But the truth is, very few people can do that. Fortunately, there's a lot of help out there now—which wasn't the case in my day. The fact you understand that you're self-medicating is a good thing, 'cos it means you ain't under any illusions, although it sounds to me like you haven't come to terms with the fact you might be an addict yet. The next stage is to find a good therapist, or a local AA meeting. That's how I started. Having said that, the most important thing for me was changing my social circle. I just don't hang out with practicing drug addicts or alcoholics any more. When you do that, you finally realize what a small minority of people have a case of beer and an eight-ball of cocaine for breakfast.

Dear Dr. Ozzy:

I'm not a big druggie, but I have a big birthday celebration coming up and I want to enjoy myself. Obviously I don't want to cause any permanent damage—or end up in hospital—so what combination of magic plants, powders, pills, and other mind-altering chemicals would you recommend for a really kick-ass time?
"David," New York

My favourite combination of drugs was pretty specific: *anything* and *anything*—and as much of it as I could get my hands on it. That pretty much guaranteed a kick-ass time...

until I woke up in prison, or in the ER, or in the middle of a twelve-lane freeway. I wish I could tell you the magic formula that'll keep you out of trouble, but I never found it. Whenever I got loaded, my self-destruct circuit activated, and I ended up trying to strangle my wife, or shoot my cats, or some other fucked-up shit. My advice? Stay clean, man.

Dr. Ozzy's Trivia Quiz: High Expectations

Find the answers—and tote up your score—on page 263

1. How can you get high from a Colorado River toad (*Bufo alvarius*)?
   a) By sucking on it
   b) By milking it, drying the venom, and smoking it
   c) By blending it and drinking the liquid

2. When a British prison inmate grew a marijuana plant in his cell, what did the wardens think it was?
   a) A tomato plant
   b) A Christmas tree
   c) A plastic ornament

3. What was Diane Linkletter high on when she jumped out of a window to her death in 1969?
   a) LSD
   b) Peyote
   c) Magic mushrooms

4. When cops raided an (alleged) meth dealer's house in Mexico City, how much cash did they find hidden in the walls?
   a) $205 million
   b) $25 million
   c) $2 billion

5. What was Operation Midnight Climax?
   a) A project to create a female instant-orgasm pill
   b) The secret nickname for Viagra drug trials
   c) A CIA-run brothel where the punters were spiked with LSD

Croaking It

12

Getting Ready for the Great Moshpit in the Sky

Knowing me, I won't leave this earth peacefully. I'll be abducted by killer turds from outer space, eaten by a giant cockroach, or crushed by a falling chunk of Halley's Comet. No matter what happens, though, one thing's for sure: my time will run out. When it comes to Death, not even the Prince of Darkness gets any special favours.

It used to bother me that I wouldn't last forever, but it doesn't any more. Don't get me wrong: I ain't planning to kick the bucket any time soon. But we're already living in an overloaded world, and it's only gonna get worse: a stray asteroid will land in the ocean, some whacked-out dictator will blow up the moon, or the next ice age will arrive. Who wants eternal life only to see all that bullshit happening? Fuck that, man: let the great-great-grandkids handle it. In the meantime, my philosophy is to make as much of what you've got, for as

long as humanly possible. So when people write to Dr. Ozzy
about getting old, that's what I tell 'em: accept the inevitable,
but don't stop.

Never stop.

Dear Dr. Ozzy:

*Is it too morbid to plan your own funeral? Or is it a thoughtful gift
for your surviving relatives, like when Peter Sellers asked for Glenn
Miller's "In the Mood" to be played during the service? (His final
joke—everyone knew he despised the song.)*

Macy, Kent

I honestly don't care what music they play at my funeral—
they can put on a medley of Justin Bieber, Susan Boyle, and
"We Are the Diddymen" if it makes 'em happy—but I *do*
want to make sure it's a celebration, not a mope-fest. I'd also
like some pranks: maybe the sound of knocking inside the
coffin; or a video of me asking my doctor for a second opinion
on his diagnosis of "death." And obviously there'll be no
harping on the bad times, like, "Oh, he was terrible boozer,
old Ozzy, and I'll never forget when he beat up the cat." So
to answer your question: yes, I do think a bit of planning is
the right thing to do for the family you leave behind. Also, it's
always worth remembering that a lot of people on this earth
see nothing but misery their whole lives. So by any measure,
most of us in the western hemisphere—especially rockers like
me—are very lucky. That's why I don't want my funeral to be
sad. I want it to be a time to say "thanks."

Dear Dr. Ozzy:

*I've reached the age when I need a walker. I can't begin to
describe to you how depressing this is. Given that you're an elder*

statesman of rock who still manages to be cool, can you tell me
how to pull off this anti-fashion accessory? (Go-faster stripes,
perhaps?)
Liv, Exeter

What do you mean, "reached the age"? They don't go, "Oh, Happy 83rd Birthday, here's a walker." My gran lived to 99 without needing any help to get around. So you've obviously got a specific problem, in which case, you've gotta do what you've gotta do, man. Paint the thing black and put a skull and crossbones on the front if it makes you feel better. Otherwise, bear in mind that Johnny Cash used a wheelchair when he got old—and even then, he was still the coolest man on the planet.

Dear Dr. Ozzy:
If you could take a test that would tell you if you're going to get
Alzheimer's in the future, would you do it?
Cherry, Boston

Sharon and I had one of those tests when we got our "genomes sequenced" (see chapter 7 for more details) and when the results were ready, we had to make that decision for real. It was a very big deal for my wife, 'cos her dad got Alzheimer's, and it was horrific. Believe me, having seen what happened to him, I wouldn't wish it on my worst fucking enemy. In his heyday, my father-in-law was one of the scariest people I'd ever met, but at the end of his life he'd been reduced to a child. Having said that, my view is that if you know about something in advance, you can do a lot to slow it down—and you might even have a chance of curing it, especially as new treatments come out over the years. Sharon feels the same way. Luckily for us, nothing in our genes suggest we're any more likely to get Alzheimer's than any other person.

Dear Dr. Ozzy:

I'm approaching my 85th birthday and have now been to more friends' funerals than I care to remember. Is it better to have an early send-off, or be the last man standing?

Dennis, Shewsbury

Unless you put a gun to head on your 65th birthday, it ain't exactly a choice you get to make, is it? Having said that, the thought of sticking around for too long seems like the worse option to me. I know a woman whose friends all died years ago, then her husband died, so she ended up living on her own...and then to top it off she got dementia. That ain't a life by anyone's definition. My own mum didn't have an easy time, either—right at the end of her life she was robbed blind by two guys who knocked on her door and told her they were from the electricity board. I've already told my wife: if it gets to the bitter end and there's an off-switch you can press, don't hesitate for one second.

DR. OZZY'S AMAZING MEDICAL MISCELLANY

Most Unlikely Ways to Die★

♦ **Hit on the head by a coconut.** Supposedly this kills 150 people every year around the world—coconuts drop from as high as 25 metres with a force of 1,000 kgs—making the odds 250 million to one. They say that being killed by a coconut is more likely than being killed by a shark. I'd still rather see a coconut above me than a fin next to me in the water.

♦ **Standing too close to an exploding toilet.** Self-explanatory, this one—and not exactly what you'd

---

*Sources: Club Direct insurance, *101 Crazy Ways to Die* by Matt Roper; National Safety Council.

want anyone writing on your death certificate. It does happen, though. Estimated odds: 340 million to one.

♦ **Legally executed.** Obviously this depends which country you're in—the odds would be zero in Britain, 'cos there's no death penalty—but in America they're 97,000 to one. Which makes it a more popular way to croak than if you were...

♦ **Bitten by a dog.** This one's a bit of a worry, given that I've got 17 of the fucking things. Luckily most of 'em are the size of tea cups. Odds: 121,000 to one.

♦ **Eaten by a cannibal.** How the fuck anyone calculated this statistic is beyond me, but the chances of ending up as someone's lunch allegedly works out at 25 billion to one. In terms of things to worry about, it's up there with being hit by an asteroid (7.5 billion to one) and being trapped in a freezer (360 million to one).

Dear Dr. Ozzy:
Suddenly, at the age of 43, I've found myself beginning to stutter. I'm mortified. Is this just a fact of getting older, or something more serious? Is it going to get worse? Please help, Dr. Ozzy.
Ellen, Birmingham

It might be serious, or it might not be, but you should go and see a neurologist, just in case. I also started to jumble my words up as I got older—although stutters run in my family. It usually happens when I'm excited or frustrated. I used to treat it with a nip of booze every now and again, which helped, until I became a raging alcoholic. By the time people saw me on *The Osbournes*, they couldn't understand a word I was saying. Then I watched the show myself, and *I* couldn't understand a word I was saying, either. You've just got to slow down. When I stopped speaking so fast, I stopped stuttering as much. I try to think of the end of a sentence now before I start it. And although I never went to a speech therapist for stuttering, I'm told that can help a lot. Why not try it?

Dear Dr. Ozzy,
I'm bald, fat and married, and becoming increasingly depressed by the thought that I'll never enjoy my wild days of youthful debauchery ever again. As someone who's given up drinking and philandering, how do you come to terms with getting old?
Mike, New Jersey

Whatever you do, don't just sit there like a lump, waiting for the Grim Reaper to arrive. Find something you enjoy doing, maybe some kind of exercise—not bonking the next-door neighbour's wife—and let off your pent-up frustration through that. Look at me: I'm 62 years old, I don't drink, I don't smoke, and I don't run around with groupies any more, but at the moment I'm doing a two-and-a-half-hour rock 'n' roll show in a different city every night, and—in my head at least—I feel like I'm 21 years old. Don't give up, man. Seriously. Accept the things you can't change and get on with your life.

DR. OZZY'S AMAZING MEDICAL MISCELLANY

Most Likely Ways to Die*

- A mind-blowing 59 million people (roughly) die every year on Planet Earth, with the most popular reason being a dodgy ticker. In fact, heart disease accounts for 12.2 per cent of all deaths throughout the world, rich and poor.

---

*Source: The World Health Organisation.

- Strokes give heart attacks a good run for their money on the Grim Reaper's Hit List, coming in at No. 2 and killing 5.7 million people a year—9.7 per cent of all deaths.
- Pneumonia and emphysema (lower respiratory infections and chronic obstructive pulmonary disease, to use the proper terms) come in at No. 3 and No. 4. Smoking is the leading cause of emphysema, another very fucking good reason to quit.
- Never in a billion years would I have guessed the fifth most common cause of death in the world: diarrhoea. Tragically, more than half of all the 2.2 million victims every year are kids under five years old, and they get it from dodgy food and water. Although it's easily treatable in the West, if you're in a poor country, a bad case of the runs can kill you from dehydration and fluid loss—especially if you're already malnourished.
- After diarrhoea, the other most likely ways to die are: AIDS (No. 6), Tuberculosis (No. 7), lung cancers (No. 8), road traffic accidents (No. 9), and premature birth/low birth weight (No. 10).

Dear Dr. Ozzy:
As the Prince of Darkness, are you a supporter of "Dr. Death"—a.k.a. the late American euthanasia advocate Jack Kevorkian, who spent almost a decade in prison?
Carlos, United States

To a certain degree I could understand "Dr. Death" when he said doctors should be able to help their patients top themselves. But then again, knowing America the way I do, if it became legal, somebody would end up doing a deal—y'know, "If you pop my nan, I'll give you 25 per cent of the inheritance" kind of thing. There are certain kinds of doctors of here—*anywhere*, probably—who'd kill you for ten grand, no problem at all. And then you'd have elderly relatives who'd feel pressured into taking the death juice, 'cos they wouldn't want to be a burden, y'know? So I'd at least want there to be some kind of process, not just squeeze-this-trigger-and-you're-gone, see ya. Having said that, though, I've always told Sharon, "If my quality of life is terrible, if I can't go for a piss by myself, if I'm paralysed—you have my permission to pull the plug." I mean, people say, "That's going against God." But *being a doctor* is going against God, isn't it? If you've got a headache, it ain't God who reaches down and gives you the aspirin.

Dear Dr. Ozzy:
At 62, you are so good-looking, man! What is your secret? Have you got some kind of magic shake that gives you eternal youth? Could you share this formula with us?
Klausitta, Tallinn, Estonia

It's called English breakfast tea, with a good brand of honey. I get through about ten bowls of that stuff a day. I also eat as much fruit as I can. Forget bowls of brown M&Ms: the first thing I ask for when I go to any hotel room on the road is a selection of the local fruit. They also say that alcohol preserves... but I don't believe that for one fucking second.

DR. OZZY'S INSANE-BUT-TRUE STORIES

The Age of the Supercentenarian

◆ When I was a kid, people counted themselves lucky if they lived long enough to get a gold watch and a retirement bash down the pub. Nowadays, you can be retired for longer than you ever worked. Take Jeanne Calment, the French chick who broke the record for the longest-ever (independently verified) human lifespan. She was born in 1875 in Arles and managed to outlive her entire family, including her grandson (he died in 1963 when he fell off a motorbike). She was so old, she'd even met Vincent van Gogh—although she thought the guy was a c***. ("Dirty, badly dressed, disagreeable...very ugly, ungracious, impolite [and] sick," was what she told one interviewer.) She was a remarkable woman, Jeanne: she took up fencing at the age of 85; kept riding a bicycle until she was 100; and smoked every day until she was 117. Meanwhile, she never went on a diet, and never stopped eating her two favourite things: olive oil and chocolate. She passed away in 1997, by which time she was an unbelievable 122 years old and 164 days. *Guinness World Records* now has a term for people like Jeanne who live beyond the age of 110: "supercentenarians." According to the experts, there are between 300 and 450 of 'em living today—and you can pretty much guarantee that number's gonna rise.

Dear Wonderful Doctor of Oz:
Now that I'm getting older, my feet constantly burn after a long day at work. I go home and rub them for two hours, thus missing **Big Brother,** *but they still ache. I'd like to hope that this isn't just the reality of age.... Have you ever had achy breaky feet?*
(Please don't say that I need feet transplants.)
Dusty, Coventry

There's an easy cure for this, Dusty: learn to walk on your hands. Give it a week, and the pain will be gone. Promise.

Dear Dr. Ozzy:
I'm getting to the age when I need to have my first prostate check-up. Do you recommend the "digital rectal exam,"

*or can I get away with the (less-intrusive) urine screening
test?*
Christian, Stoke Newington, London

I don't care if it's a blood test, a urine test, or if they have to stick
a bicycle frame up there—*get it done.* I've lost too many friends to
prostate cancer to worry about any temporary discomfort.

Dear Dr. Ozzy:
*My 92-year-old mother is becoming unbearable. She's in good
enough shape to live by herself but relies on me for almost 24/7
support, making it impossible for me to enjoy my retirement with
my husband while we're still both in good health. Even if we go
away for a weekend, she calls day and night, laying on the emotional
blackmail. What can do?*
Anne, Cumbria

Here's the problem with hanging on to your marbles for
so long: you end up becoming very aware of how difficult,
lonely, and painful your life is getting—and it doesn't put
you in a very good mood. I've personally never had to deal
with that kind of situation, 'cos both my parents died quite
young, and my father-in-law had Alzheimer's, which meant
he didn't have a clue what time of day it was. As heavy-duty
as Alzheimer's is, I sometimes wonder if that's the better way
to go. But y'know, there's no getting away from the fact that
modern medicine has created a whole new set of issues when
it comes to people living to these crazy ages—and I don't
think we're anywhere near getting to the bottom of them.
My only advice is to go to your doctor, tell him (or her) that
this situation is gonna send you to the loony bin, and find out
what kind of extra help might be available. Even if you have
to pay for a private nurse out of your own pocket, it might be
worth it. As you say, *you* ain't gonna live forever, either.

Dr. Ozzy's Trivia Quiz: Meet the Worms

Find the answers—and tote up your score—on page 263

1. For a fee, a U.S. company will turn your cremated remains into...
   a) Stained glass
   b) A salad bowl (with optional tongs)
   c) A diamond

2. What's a "Sky burial"?
   a) When your ashes are blasted into outer space on a Russian-made rocket
   b) When your corpse is fed to vultures
   c) When your ashes are thrown out of a plane over your favourite place

3. Which of these Last Will & Testaments are real?
   a) The Australian bloke who left one shilling to his wife—"for a tram fare so she can go somewhere and drown herself"
   b) The Beverly Hills socialite who asked to be buried in her Ferrari, wearing a lace gown, "with the seat slanted comfortably"
   c) The Countess who left $80 million to her dog

4. What did Duke Ferdinand of Brunswick demand to have in his coffin?
   a) A window
   b) An air tube
   c) A lid he could unlock and open—allowing him to walk out into his tomb if he "woke up" (the key was to be put in his shroud pocket)

5. "Angel Lust" is what, exactly?
   a) When a corpse gets a boner
   b) When someone wishes for an early death
   c) When someone turns religious on their death
      bed

Dr. Ozzy's Prescription Pad

Epilogue

Take as Directed...

As much as this book ain't supposed to be taken too seriously, I hope you've learned a few things along the way—I know *I* have. When people ask you for advice every week, it's liking getting a crash course in human nature. You also learn a lot about yourself in a weird kind of way. So before I sign-off, here are a ten simple tips I've come up with over my time as "Dr. Ozzy" for living a long and happy life. They won't solve *every* problem. But I promise you: keep 'em in mind, and you'll at least have a shot at avoiding some of the stupid fucking mistakes I've made over the years.

God bless you all.
Dr. Ozzy

- Your doctor has seen patients come through his doors with fluorescent green dicks and/or family pets stuck up their buttholes, so *trust me*, whatever's wrong with you ain't as embarrassing as you think it is.

- If you think it might be the booze, *it's the booze.*
- No-one's family is perfect. Worry about *real* problems, not about what other people think.
- If you find a lump—*any* lump—don't prick it with a pin, hit it with a mallet, look it up on the internet, or ask Dr. Ozzy if you should wait until it grows into a second head. Get it checked out, now. (And get a physical every year.)
- Your genes don't decide who you are—*you* do. If the Prince of Darkness managed to get clean and sober after 40 years, anything is fucking possible.
- People who make you feel bad about yourself ain't your real friends.
- Most of us are fucking lunatics, one way or another. Some just hide it better than others.
- If you write to Dr. Ozzy to ask if something is right or wrong...you know it's wrong.
- All drugs are basically the same—booze, pot, cocaine, heroin...whatever. They're just different ways to escape from life. So before asking me if "a little bit" of this or that is safe in moderation, here's my answer: do it if you want to, man, but don't kid yourself. You ain't kidding anyone else.
- Always get a second opinion—even if that means calling your doctor on a cell phone from six feet underground to ask him if he's 100 per cent sure you're dead.

Quiz Answers

Dr. Ozzy's advice column appears every week in
The Sunday Times and in select issues of *Rolling Stone*

Write to Dr. Ozzy:
askdrozzy@sunday-times.co.uk
Quiz Answers

*Award yourself one point for each correct answer, add up your
total score, then see how you did on page 274...*

MAGIC MEDICINE

1. b). I ain't kidding—you can even look up the *British Medical Journal* paper online. The scientists said they wanted "to assess the effects of didgeridoo playing on daytime sleepiness...by reducing collapsibility of the upper airways in patients with moderate obstructive sleep apnoea syndrome and snoring." And I thought *my* job was fucking ridiculous.

2. a). They turn the poor old frog into juice by dropping it in a blender (they kill it and skin it first). They also spice it up with "white bean broth," honey, raw aloe vera, and maca

(an Andean root thing). If throwing up gives you a raging boner, it probably works a treat.

3. c). Makes sense, I suppose, 'cos bats have amazing night vision. Still, as one of the few people on this planet who have actually swallowed bat's blood, I can vouch that it doesn't have any special powers—otherwise I wouldn't have needed cataract surgery in 2010.

4. a). This a terrible myth, 'cos it's been used to justify rape, and it makes the disease spread much faster.

5. b). Not much of a surprise, this one. In the 1960s everyone tried to cure everything with LSD.

Health Nut

1. a). They call it "fat" for a reason. One tablespoon of the stuff has about 120 calories, compared with 112 for ghee and 101 for butter (according to Nutrientfacts.com and Fitday.com).

2. All three. Or at least that's the advice of a weird-sounding organisation called the National Digestive Diseases Information Clearinghouse. It says you can swallow less air by not chewing gum, eating your meals slower, and making sure your false choppers fit right.

3. a). The poor fucker who did the field work to come up with this number deserves the Victoria Cross, if you ask me (he works for the NDDIC, as above). But thank God this kind of information exists, 'cos next time I'm feeling intimidated by someone, I'll remind myself that they burped or let their arse cheeks blow 14 times in the previous 24 hours.

4. b) and c). If you overdo it when you're training, you can end up feeling like you're wading through molten lead. When that happens, you've gotta slow down and see a doc, or you

can do yourself some serious damage. Pregnant women and overweight people can also get heavy legs—as can anyone who stands or sits in the same position for too long.

5. b). The guy was so tough-as-nails, he never even warmed up before exercising. "Does a lion warm up when he's hungry?" he once said. "No! He just goes out there and eats the sucker." (Unlike LaLanne, Dr. Ozzy recommends frequent stretching.)

BEING BEAUTIFUL

1. a) and b). If you believe what you read on the internet, Cleopatra also used crocodile turds as a contraceptive. Hence the old Egyptian chat-up line, "Wanna come back to my place and see my dung?"

2. All three. They were recommended as baldness cures for Julius Caesar, who also tried to compensate for his thinning rug by going out and buying himself a red convertible chariot.

3. c). Generally speaking, if your car windows don't have special UV protection, they'll block most UVB rays—which tan and burn you the most—but not UVA rays, which give you wrinkles and cause so-called "commuter ageing."

4. c). The Sultan of Brunei (according to *The Sunday Times*). He flew his barber from the Dorchester Hotel in Mayfair to Brunei (7,000 miles) and gave him a private suite on Singapore Airlines to make sure he didn't catch swine flu on the way. Seems perfectly sensible to me.

5. a). Which shouldn't exactly come as a fucking surprise if you've ever been to the Czech Republic. The first "beer spa" opened at a brewery in Chodovz Plana, near Prague, back in 2006.

Flesh & Blood

1. b). His brothers did it 'cos they were jealous. They also nicked his coat and threw him down a mineshaft. They didn't let him play their Xbox, either.

2. c). The mother was supposedly a Russian peasant, married to a guy named Feodor Vassilyev (her first name has been lost to history). According to *Guinness World Records*, she pumped out sixteen pairs of twins, seven sets of triplets, and four sets of quadruplets between 1725 and 1765. Only two of the babies died in infancy. Feodor—otherwise known as the man with the Golden Balls—went on to re-marry and have another twenty kids.

3. a). According to news reports at the time, the victim (who wasn't named) didn't realise what had happened until she noticed a wet feeling under her shirt, pulled it up, and her nipple fell on the floor. She put it a bag and took it to hospital. It's now back where it belongs.

4. c). "Marriage should be about losing arguments and winning relationships," according to Rabbi Shmuley Boteach, a leading relationship coach.

5. c). Lina Medina's parents took her to hospital, thinking she had a stomach tumor. It turned out she was seven months pregnant. She's now in her seventies and lives in Peru. The reason Lina was able to have a kid was her very unusual case of "precocious puberty"—her first period came when she was still a toddler—although of course it's beyond tragic that any man would impregnate her in the first place. The father was never identified, and the baby, a boy, was raised as her brother. He died in 1979 at the age of 40.

Under the Knife

1. a) and c). The guy with the forked tongue—Erik Sprague—had it done on purpose, 'cos he wanted to look like a lizard. He had his teeth filed into fangs, too. He's available for babysitting.

2. a) and c). The woman who injected lubricant into her face told ABC News: "By the following day [my whole face] was just completely inflamed. [The lubricant] expands, it's like rubber, and your own collagen forms scar tissue around it...it looked like horrible blisters." People who do this kind of thing to themselves suffer from a condition called "body dysmorphic disorder"—which means they drive themselves nuts about one particular part of their body, to the point where they're willing to self-operate.

3. b). The *Annals of General Psychiatry* says that "severe intentional eye self-injury is uncommon, but not rare" and that it's usually a result of a drug freak-out psychosis, bipolar disorder, obsessive compulsive disorder, post-traumatic stress disorder, and/or depression. Some patients have been found with a copy of the passage in Matthew's Gospel, which says, "...if the right eye offends thee, pluck it out and cast it from thee."

4. a). They were known as "barber surgeons." The most common service they provided was "bloodletting"—where you cut a gash in your arm and let your blood run out into a bucket. Personally, I'd have been happy with a short back and sides.

5. a). The poor guy, who was 70 years old and mentally ill, died from septicaemia within six days. The others are real cases written about in *The Psychiatrist*, although the bright spark with the bicycle changed his mind at the last minute—and ended up fracturing his skull instead.

Doctor! Doctor!

1. a). He was sacked and fined for making out prescriptions to himself, then booked himself into rehab. He wasn't struck off, though—and he went on to kill over 200 patients, that we know of, at least.
2. a). The woman later withdrew her case and the doc was exonerated.
3. b). He went to jail. He allegedly told one woman that his magic potion would stop her gums bleeding, but warned it might "taste funny." He also told her she could swallow it if she wanted to.
4. c). "I hope that what I've done will reassure men that vasectomies can be relatively pain free," he told the BBC. He added that he'd been thinking of getting the snip for a while, but wanted someone trustworthy to do it. "Eventually I just thought, 'sod it, I'll do it myself," he said.
5. c). The Gallup poll came out in 2010 and showed just how much dough gets spent on "defensive medicine"— basically, doctors covering their own arses in case a patient takes 'em to the cleaners.

Mutant Strains

1. a). When the bones of tiny, hobbit-like creatures were found on a remote Indonesian island, Flores, some scientists thought they might have been humans with a crazy genetic disorder who lived 18,000 years ago. Others said they were a different species altogether.
2. a) and b). Although it looked like she had four arms and four legs, she was actually *two* people. After a mind-blowing 27-hour operation, little Lakshmi—who was

worshipped as a Hindu Goddess by some Indians—now goes to school and can walk on her own. The poor kid still needs more surgery, though.

3. a) I almost fell out of my fucking chair when my research guy told me about this. It ain't the antifreeze you put in your car, mind you, but an "antifreeze protein" found in certain Antarctic fish that stops 'em dying from the cold. They've even started to use the stuff in some low-fat ice creams—although it's grown in a lab, not taken directly out of some smelly old flounder.

4. c). An Austrian monk called Gregor Mendel had the mega-brainwave that led to modern genetics after growing and studying 29,000 pea plants between 1856 and 1863. He didn't get any recognition during his lifetime, but at least he never went hungry in the lab.

5. b). Said one of the scientists who cloned her: "Dolly is derived from a mammary gland cell, and we couldn't think of a more impressive pair of glands than Dolly Parton's."

Personal Skills

1. c). I'm told the other two greetings work in Oman (nose kiss) and some parts of Niger ("Wooshay!")—but always double-check before giving a strange foreign bloke a smacker on the conk.

2. c). "Don't put your phone on the dining table, or glance at it longingly mid-conversation," it says. Other rules: don't make calls from the shitter; don't have phone conversations in public about money, sex, or your haemorrhoid attack; and think carefully before choosing "My Humps" as a ringtone.

3. a). Not that I'd know—I don't have the first fucking clue about computers. Experts say the human brain can only

handle a maximum number of 150 *real* friends, so if you've got more than that, you might wanna take advantage of National Unfriend Day (November 17).

4. b). During the heist—which the boss helped to plan—his employees were held at knifepoint and one teller was punched in the face. The boss pretended to be a hostage until the cops showed up and realised that one of the masked robbers was his girlfriend.

5. a). "There were problems with money in the workplace and basically the stress of him being the owner and running a business got to him," said the cops.

GREY MATTER

1. All of them. a) is also known as "muscle dysmorphia," 'cos sufferers never think they look "ripped" enough, b) is usually caused by a major brain injury, and c) is described by experts as an "exaggerated startle reflex"—in other words, you pretty much crap your pants when you're surprised. Weirdly, it was first discovered in French-Canadian lumberjacks living in Maine, USA.

2. a). It means you're turned on by people who commit crimes. It's also known as "Bonnie and Clyde Syndrome."

3. a). I ain't exactly a brain surgeon, but I'm told that's more or less true (apparently headaches come from blood vessels, the membrane around the brain, and other nerves). If you're ever unlucky enough to have brain surgery, you can even get away with just a local anaesthetic on your scalp. As for the other two answers: your brain could power only a 10-23w bulb; and the biggest emotional memory trigger is thought to be smell.

4. b). That's what the scientist Stephen Juan said in his 1998 book *The Odd Brain*. Most thoughts are turned into very

short-term memories and then forgotten. Or make that "all thoughts" in my case.

5. c). That makes 'em the most commonly prescribed drugs in the country—after high blood pressure medication (according to a 2005 report from the Centers for Disease Control and Prevention).

SEXY BEAST

1. a). The serotonin released when you bonk is like nature's aspirin, according to one specialist, Dr. Vincent Martin— who was recently voted the Best Doctor in the World by married men everywhere.

2. c). Diphallia means you're born with two dicks (one usually bigger than the other). It ain't exactly common, though: there have been only 100 cases since the first one was discovered in 1609.

3. c). The "buyer"—a 38-year-old Australian business-man, if you believe what you read in the press—backed out at the last minute 'cos his wife found out. It still ain't clear if he got his $250,000 deposit back. The whole thing was a PR stunt organised by a knocking shop in Nevada.

4. b). The festival is held every year on March 15—and everyone gets blasted on sake. The guys who carry the giant dick have to be exactly 42 years old, 'cos it's believed to be an unlucky age.

5. a). The beauty contest is known as the Gerewol and happens every September, with the guys trying to show off their height and the whiteness of their eyes and teeth. As if that weren't freaky enough, they also get out of their minds on a drink made of psychoactive bark.

HIGH EXPECTATIONS

1. a). If you milk the venom and dry it out, you end up with a drug called bufotenine, which—when smoked—gives you the same kind of high as LSD. *Don't* try it, though, 'cos it's illegal (and the toads are endangered). A former Scout leader in California is one of the few people who've ever been arrested for taking a "toad trip." He told agents that his mind was blown so wide open, he could "hear electrons jumping orbitals in my molecules."

2. a) and b). The gold-toothed criminal managed to grow the pot plant for five months at Verne Prison in Dorset—he even hung tinsel on it during Christmas—before the screws finally realised that the mile-wide grin on his face wasn't 'cos his heirlooms were so ripe.

3. None of them, according to the autopsy. Her famous dad, Art, blamed a flashback from LSD—which lead to the theory that people think they can fly when they're freaking out on acid.

4. a). They also found "eight luxury vehicles, seven weapons, and a machine to make pills." The alleged dealer, a Chinese guy, was later arrested in the U.S.

5. c). It was part of the CIA's insane MK-Ultra mind-control programme in the 1950s and 1960s. Punters were lured into a brothel in San Francisco, then drugged and sexually blackmailed while agents sat behind two-way glass, taking notes. The CIA thought the Johns would be too embarrassed to complain to the cops the next morning. They were right.

MEET THE WORMS

1. c). LifeGem takes carbon from human remains and uses it to make synthetic diamonds. In 2007, the company made

a diamond partly from carbon extracted from 10 strands of Ludwig van Beethoven's hair: it was sold on eBay for $202,700 (the money went to charity).

2. b). Tibetans used to do this 'cos most of 'em are Buddhists and think the human body is an "empty vessel" after death. Also, Tibet is a rocky place, so digging graves is a major ballache—and cremation would use up scarce firewood. There are some crazy pictures on the internet of "body-breakers" cutting up corpses while vultures queue up for their dinner.

3. All of 'em. The Ferrari woman was Sandra Ilene West, who died at 37 from a drug overdose. The car—a powder blue 1964 Ferrari 330 America—was put in a wooden box and covered with concrete (to make sure no-one nicked it) and lowered into a hole nine feet under the Alamo Masonic Cemetery in Texas. For organising the burial, her brother-in-law was given a $2 million inheritance. If he'd refused to do it, he would have got only $10,000.

4. All three. This happened in the 1700s when "safety coffins" were all the rage after a few horrendous cases of people being buried alive. Other coffin designs had cords attached to church bells, so you could sound the alarm if you "woke up." The only problem: bodies usually swell up and move as they decompose—so on more than one occasion, a fresh corpse in the churchyard ended up ringing the bell, scaring the shit out of the Vicar.

5. a). A "death erection" usually happens after being hung, shot in the head, or poisoned (it's technically known as a "priapism" and you can also get it with a severe spinal chord injury, I'm told). If Mother Nature had any mercy, she'd give you the boner *before* you died.

How did you score?

41-60: Medical genius. If haven't tried brain surgery yet, now might be the time.

21-40: Hypochondriac. You have just enough knowledge to be a danger to yourself and society.

0-20: Medical liability. You're so clueless, you could end up accidentally stabbing yourself in the kidney while clipping your toenails. Wear Bubble Wrap and remain indoors at all times.